A DIALOGUE WITH THE
GHOSTS
of RESISTANCE

A DIALOGUE WITH THE
GHOSTS
of RESISTANCE

Howard Thurman, Education, the Oppressed and the
Civil Rights Movement: How and Why Protest Succeed:
A Historical Biography and a Memoir
for My Beloved Wife

M . S H A R P E

CITI OF
BOOKS

CITIOFBOOKS, INC.
3736 Eubank NE Suite A1
Albuquerque, NM 87111-3579
www.citiofbooks.com
Hotline: 1 (877) 389-2759
Fax: 1 (505) 930-7244

Ordering Information:
Quantity sales. Special discounts are available on quantity purchases by corporations, associations, and others. For details, contact the publisher at the address above.

Printed in the United States of America.

ISBN-13:	Softcover	979-8-89391-753-6
	eBook	979-8-89391-754-3

Library of Congress Control Number: 2025912478

TABLE OF CONTENTS

"A Dialogue with the Ghosts of Resistance: Howard Thurman, Education, the Oppressed and the Civil Rights Movement: How Protests Succeed": Black Studies as Historical Biography and a Memoir For My Beloved:

M. Sharpe

"What happens to a dream deferred? Does it dry up like a raisin in the sun? Or fester like a sore---and then run? Does it stink like rotten meat? Or crust and sugar over--like syrup. Maybe it just sags like a heavy load. Or does it explode?"

Langston Hughes

"Though we would like to live without regrets, and sometimes proudly insist that we have none, this is not possible, if only because we are mortal"

James Baldwin

"We're ready. We're prepared. Do not give into fear. We are fearless. This is not the rime to be afraid. This is the time to stand up and fight back, and to resist any temptation for them to divide us. We're in this together. The rule of law is on our side. We will not give in, we will not give up, we will not capitulate, we will not bow, we will not bend...we will survive!"

Ketanji Brown Jackson

"America believes education to be dangerous. And America is not wholly wrong. For education always has had, and always will have, an element of danger, of dissatisfaction, of discontent and of revolution. Nevertheless, the educated strives to know."

W.E.B. Du Bois

AUTOBIOGRAPHY

Malcolm X remarked, "The moment you decide to question the story you become dangerous. You see, education is not memorizing what someone in power wrote in a textbook. Education is the process of reclaiming one's own thinking." Howard Thurman remarked, "Finally, I understood what my high school meant by education is the "gold key."" I was raised in one of the many neglected corners of America—where poverty, segregation, and systemic neglect were everyday realities. But from that space also came strength. I was fortunate to be guided by those who gave everything they had so I could stand where I am standing today. Being and becoming the first in my family to complete graduate education was not just a personal milestone—it was part of a longer, collective journey. Therefore, I am a Black Studies researcher and writer whose work dwells at the intersection of protest, grief, memory, and spiritual resistance. I write from an academic and a personal place of enduring love, lived experience, and academic conviction. Howard Thurman remarked, "I share with you the agony of your grief. The anguish of your heart finds echo in my own. I know I cannot enter into all you feel, nor bear with you the burden of your pain. I can but offer what my love does give: strength of caring, the warmth of one who seeks to understand the silent storm-swept barrenness of so great a loss. This I do in quiet ways, that on your lonely path you may not walk alone." This book, 'A Dialogue with the Ghosts of Resistance, is not merely a historical study—it is also a memoir, a reckoning, and in many ways, an act of survival after the death of "My Beloved."

ACKNOWLEDGEMENTS

Howard Thurman remarked, "I must express my deepest appreciation to a group of friends who built the fire underneath this pot and waited patiently for it to boil. They requested anonymity and of course they shall have it but let them read here that I shall never forget them." This book pays tribute to the Howard Thurman, whose voice still echoes in the heart of spiritual resistance, and it honors those who encouraged and supported me during this writing journey whom I have decided to keep anonymous out of reverence. But what I offer in these pages is real: my grief, grief and my inquiry into "A Dialogue with the Ghosts of Resistance."

CHAPTER 1

THE PROBLEM OF ERASING HISTORY

Maulana Karenga wrote in "Introduction to Black Studies" (University of Sankore Press: 1982/2010), "'Black studies' is a specialized branch of study and knowledge....Black studies is the critical and systematic study of the thought and practice of Black lives in their current and historical unfolding." Maulana Karenga wrote in "Introduction to Black Studies" (University of Sankore Press: 1982/2010), "It is critical in that it is characterized by careful analysis and considered judgment. And it is systematic in that it is structured and methodical in its pursuit and presentation of knowledge..." Further, Jacqueline Bobo et al wrote in "The Black Studies Reader" (Routledge: 2004), edited by Jacqueline Bobo et al, "Black Studies, as a socially engaged field of scholarly inquiry, is the progeny of centuries of research that seeks to redress long-standing misconceptions of Black inferiority, African heritage, and cultural significance."

Noam Chomsky remarked, "Something dangerous is about to hit America. And you can feel it in the air, like the quiet before the storm. It doesn't matter what shape it takes...economic turmoil, political upheaval, technological disruption or a crisis we haven't yet imagined." A recent "AI Overview: The Deportation of Black Lives in America" (2025), "Several recent reports indicate that the proposed or implemented policies that could have a significant impact on Black lives in America, including those related to deportation. Here's a summary of the situation:1. Deportation rhetoric and plans. There is repeatedly expressed interest in deporting individuals with criminal records, including those born in the US, and has suggested exploring the legality of sending them to foreign countries like El Salvador. While deporting US citizens is unconstitutional under current law, could lay the groundwork for mass deportation efforts, potentially including those with dual nationalities or tenuous citizenship records.

Maurice Waite wrote in "Paperback Oxford English Dictionary" (Oxford: 2102), "The concepts, "erase," "erased" and "erasure," is defined as "the actions, activities, behaviors, conduct and events of rubbing something out with the conscious aim, goal and intent of removing all traces of." Jason Stanley wrote in "How Fascism Works" (Random House: 2018), "Fascist politics invokes a pure mythic past tragically destroyed. Depending on how the nation is defined, the mythic past may be religiously pure, racially pure, culturally pure, or all of the above...." In "Erasing History: How Fascists Rewrite the Past to Control the Future" (Atrium: 2024), Jason Stanley wrote, "Mussolini makes clear that the fascist mythic past is intentionally mythical. The function of the mythic past, in fascist politics, is to harness the emotion of nostalgia to the central tenets of fascist ideology — authoritarianism, hierarchy, purity, and struggle...." Further, Jason Stanley wrote in "How Fascism Works" (Random House: 2018), "The erasure of a nation's past is characteristic of a fascist regime." Jason Stanley wrote in "Erasing History: How Fascists Rewrite the Past to Control the Future" (Atrium: 2024), "The erasing of the Black history of protest and resistance is used to pave the way for the continuation of power and oppression. When you represent — when you erase the Black history of protest and resistance, you represent American history as just the exploits of great white men. We justify, legitimize, rationalize and sanction the "Great White Replacement Theory," which is a core message that the greatness of a patriotic America comes from the exploits of great white men, and so we need to protect that white identity."

Furthermore, Ann Hill Bond wrote in "A Morehouse Student Was Lynched in 1930: Why the College Gave Him a Posthumous Degree" Atlanta Capital News.org (02 June 2025), "We have another lynching victim to remember," said Allison Bantimba, former leader for the Fulton County Remembrance Coalition. "And I'd like you to take the lead on this remembrance because of your connection and reverence to Atlanta's history." Ann Hill Bond wrote in "A Morehouse Student Was Lynched in 1930: Why the College Gave Him a Posthumous Degree" Atlanta Capital News.org (02 June 2025), "This wasn't the first lynching report I'd received — I've read many over the years — but Dennis Hubert's story was different. Like Warren Powell, who was just 14 years old when he was lynched in East Point, Georgia, in 1899, Dennis was a child to some and a young man to others. Dennis was 18— a divinity student at Morehouse College. A son and grandson...."

Ann Hill Bond wrote in "Black Historical Erasure: A Critical Comparative Analysis in Rosewood and Ocoee Massacres", Rollins College.edu (Spring 2020), Christelle Ram wrote, "The phenomena of the erasure of Black history occur on a nationwide scale. Formally referred to as erasure, according to literary analysts, this happening is particularly relevant to the South and to the United States as a whole. The question of Black history in America is both contentious and scandalous. History, for many white persons, is a point of pride. For Black lives, Black history exemplifies the struggle with inequality, inequity, injustice and unfairness. The endeavor towards the historical recognition of the struggles of Black lives both during chattel enslavement slavery and during the violence during and following Reconstruction has lasted centuries, made difficult by the governmental and hegemonic and cultural institutions that lack both the power and willingness to grapple and accurately portray Black historical events in America."

Moreover, John J. Tierney, Jr., wrote in "Erasing History" Institute of World Politics" (26 April 2019), "America has long been known as "ahistorical" (indifferent), but it also has demonstrated signs of being deliberately "anti-historical" (opposed to historical understanding)." Anja Berniger wrote in "Erasing History as a Form of Defensive Forgetting" Wiley Online Library (01 Dec 2024), "I suggest that sometimes societies aim to forget history for defensive reasons (i.e. to cover up past wrongdoing)."

In "Why the Erasure of History Matters" BESA Center Perspectives (07 Sept 2020), Dr. Asaf Romirowsky wrote, "If one is to understand the present, one has to document the historical periods that preceded it." In

"Towards Erasure Studies: Excavating the Material Conditions of Memory and Forgetting" Memory, Mind & Media (2023), Johan Fredrikson and Chris Haffenden wrote, "While the history and practices of collecting have received considerable attention over the past few decades, the notion of erasure – of the deleting, removal or destruction of the material history of the oppressed whether deliberate or otherwise – has remained largely in the shadows....This article draws upon a recent turn to consider questions of forgetting, ignorance and ending the material history of the oppressed, and to lay out the grounds for analyzing the various roles played by the erasure of history in making and unmaking our American world." In "Historical Amnesia" Journal of Public and Progressional Sociology (September 2012), Melvyn L. Fein wrote, "Schools have apparently not done a good job in informing Americans of the country's history and hence they do not know the realities....it seems to me that American historical amnesia is commonplace." Frederick Douglas remarked in "What To The Slave Is Your Fourth of July?" Rochester, New York (05 July 1852), "We have to do with the past only as we can make it useful to the present and to the future in America." In "The Propaganda of History" in "Black Reconstruction" (Oxford: 1935/2010), W.E.B. Du Bois wrote, "How the facts of history have been falsified because the nation was ashamed. The South was ashamed because it fought to perpetuate human slavery. The North was ashamed because it had to call in the black men to save the Union, abolish slavery and establish democracy."

George Santayana remarked, "Those who cannot remember the past are condemned to repeat it." Ronald Wright remarked, "Each time history repeats itself; the price goes up." Syndey J. Harris remarked, "History repeats itself, but in such cunning disguise that we never detect the resemblance until the damage is done." Further, Chuck Palahniuk remarked, "There are only patterns, patterns on top of patterns, patterns that affect other patterns. Patterns hidden by patterns. Patterns within patterns. If you watch closely, history does nothing but repeat itself. What we call chaos is just patterns we haven't recognized. What we call random is just patterns we can't decipher. What we can't understand we call nonsense. What we can't read we call gibberish. There is no free will. There are no variables." In "Lies My Teacher Told Me" CBSD. org (2017), James W. Loewen wrote, "Textbooks almost never use the present to illuminate the past. Conversely, textbooks seldom use the past to illuminate the present. They portray the past as a simple-minded morality play. "Be good in " is the message that textbooks extract from the past. "You have a proud heritage. Be all that you can be. After all, look at what the United States has accomplished!" In sum, startling errors of omission and distortion mar American histories."

In addition, James W. Loewen wrote in "Lies My Teacher Told Me" CBSD.org (2017), "When American history textbooks leave out....and omit Black American history they offend Black American lives...." For example, on the one hand, Howard Thurman wrote in "On Viewing the Coast of Africa" (Pacifica Gallery: 1957), "From my cabin window I look out on the full moon, and the ghosts of my forefathers rise and fall with the undulating waves. Across these same waters, how many years ago they came! What were the inchoate mutterings locked tight within the circle of their hearts? In the deep heavy darkness of the foul-smelling hold of the ship, where they could not see the sky, nor hear the night noises, nor feel the warm compassion of the tribe, they held their breath against the agony. How does the human spirit accommodate itself to desolation? How did they do they/ What tools of the spirit were in their hands with which to cut a path through the wilderness of their despair?... Nothing anywhere in all the myths, in all the stories, in all the ancient memories of the race, had given any hint of this tortuous convulsion. There were no gods to hear, no magic spell of witch doctor to summon; even one's companion in chains muttered his quivering misery in a tongue unknown and a sound unfamiliar. O my fathers, what was it like to be stripped of all support of life save the beating of the heart and the ebb and flow of fetid air in the lungs?"

On the other hand, in "The Search for Common Ground" (Harper & Row: 1971), Howard Thurman wrote, "Unlike the American Indian, the African slave was uprooted from his land, his territory, and forcibly brought forcibly several thousand miles away to another land completely alien to his spirit and his gods. All ties that gave him a sense of belonging, of counting, of being a person nourished by a community of people were abruptly severed, lacerated, torn asunder. Bodies that were emotionally bleeding hulks were set down in the new world of the Americas. Initially he had no standing, even that of an outsider. In terms of his access to the sources of nourishment for the community, initially he had none. No, not even the status of being a human being. It is no accident that the New Testament Greek word for slave is "soma," which means "body, a thing."

5

CHAPTER 2
THE PROBLEM OF EDUCATION

Nelson Mandela remarked, "When it comes to the oppressed, education is the most powerful weapon which you can use to the world." Carl Sagan wrote in "The Demon-Haunted World: Science as a Candle in the Dark" (Ballantine Books: 1995/1997), "I have a foreboding of America ....when the dumbing down of America is most evident in the slow decay of substantive content in the enormously influential media, the 30-second sound bites now down to 10 seconds or less, lowest-common-denominator programming, credulous presentations on pseudoscience and superstition, but especially a kind of celebration of ignorance." In "How Fascism Works" (Random House: 2018), Jason Stanley wrote. "Universities are the canary in the coal mine of fascism." A recent "AI Overview: The Concept of Canary in a Coal Mine" (2025) wrote, "The concept, "canary in a coal mine," is an idiom that refers to something which serves as a warning of potential danger or trouble. The phrase originates from the historical practice of coal miners taking canaries into mines to detect toxic gases like "carbon monoxide." Canaries are more sensitive to these gases than humans, so if a canary died, it signaled to miners that the air was unsafe, and they needed to evacuate."

Concerning W.E.B. Du Bois, Historically Black Colleges as institutions (HBCUs) and education, Arthur Schopenhauer remarked, "The intelligent are condemned for seeing what others refuse to see." For instance, W.E.B. Du Bois wrote in "Dusk of Dawn" (Oxford: 1940/2018), "There is but one coward on earth, and that is the coward that dare not know." In "Institutions, Institutional Change and Economic Performance" (Cambridge Univ. Press: 2012), "Institutions, together with the standard\ constraints of economic theory, determine the opportunities in a society. Organizations are created to take advantage of those opportunities, and, as the organizations evolve, they alter institutions. The resultant path of institutional change is shaped by (1) the lock-in that comes from the symbiotic relationship between institutions and the organizations that have evolved as a consequence of the incentive structure provided by those institutions and (2) the feedback process by which human beings perceive and react to changes in the opportunity set."

Douglas North wrote in "Institutions, Institutional Change and Economic Opportunity" (Cambridge Univ. Press: 1990), "Institutions determine the opportunities in a society." Douglas North wrote in "Institutions, Institutional Change and Economic Opportunity" (Cambridge Univ. Press: 1990), " Institutions are the rules of the game. Institutions structure the interconnectedness of attitudes, beliefs, discourse, actions, activities and behavior of mutually interdependent human beings who reside in human communities of oppression...." Derrick White wrote in "An Independent Approach to Black Studies" :Journal of African American Studies (March 2012), "There is an impressive roster of intellectual activists who were products of the Civil Rights Movement and the Black Power Human Rights Movement and the cauldron of student activism....scholars of the history of Black Studies have not fully investigated the history of protest movements" and their intimate educational relationships to and with the institutions referred to as Historically Black Colleges and Universities (HBCUs).

For example, it is now well known that many of the leaders and student- leaders in the Civil Rights Movement either attended and/ or graduated from institutions, commonly referred to as Historically Black College and University's (HBCUs). It is also now well known that Howard Thurman also attended and graduated at the top of his class from Morehouse College, which is also an institution commonly referred to as Historically Black College or University (HBCU), which had a profound direct and indirect influence upon leaders. as well as student leaders and children in the Civil Rights Movement.

Why and how did Howard Thurman provide a profound direct and indirect influence upon leaders as well as student-leaders and children in the Civil Rights Movement? The theory here is that Howard Thurman had a profound direct and indirect influence upon leaders, as well as student-leaders and children in the Civil Rights Movement.

Maurice Craft wrote in "Education and Cultural Pluralism" (Routledge: 1984/2018), "There are two different Latin words for the concept of education. They are "educare" and "educere," meaning to accompany out, to bring out, to escort out, to guide out, and to lead out."

Lucius T. Outlaw Jr., wrote in "Africana Philosophy," in "The Stanford Encyclopedia of Philosophy" (Fall 2022), "The concept, "Africana philosophy (Black Studies)" is the name for an emergent and still developing field of ideas and idea-spaces, intellectual endeavors, discourses, and discursive networks within and beyond academic philosophy that was recognized as such by national and international organizations of professional philosophers, including the American Philosophical Association, starting in the 1980s. Thus, the name does not refer to a particular philosophy, philosophy, method, or tradition. Rather, "Africana philosophy" (Black Studies) is a third-order, meta-philosophical, umbrella-concept used to bring organizing oversight to various efforts of "philosophizing"—that is, actions, activities, behaviors and events of reflective, critical thinking and articulation and aesthetic expression—engaged in by persons and peoples African and of African American descent who were and are indigenous residents of continental Africa and residents of the many African Diasporas worldwide. In all cases the point of much of the philosophizing has been to confer meaningful orderings on individual and shared living and on natural and social worlds while resolving recurrent, emergent, and "radically" disruptive challenges to existence so as to survive, endure, and flourish across successive generations."

Howard Thurman wrote in "With Head and Heart: The Autobiography of Howard Thurman" (Harcourt Brace Jovanovich:

1979), "Now, I understood what my high school teacher meant by "education is the gold key."" Moreover, Howard Thurman wrote in "With Head and Heart: The Autobiography of Howard Thurman" (Harcourt Brace Jovanovich: 1979), "Each instructor at Morehouse College made his special contribution to the direction our lives would take. We were committed to the mission Morehouse College inculcated in us. Our job was to learn so that we could go back to our communities and teach others." In addition, Howard Thurman wrote in "With Head and Heart: The Autobiography of Howard Thurman" (Harcourt Brace Jovanovich: 1979), "The library was my refuge and my joy for the first time I had hundreds, nay thousands of books at my disposal....at last, the world of books was mine for the asking." Similarly, Malcolm X remarked," My Alma Mater was books, a good library... I could spend the rest of my life reading, just satisfying my curiosity." In "Literacy as the Path to Freedom: How Slave Owners Purposefully Kept Enslaved Black Lives Illiterate" Reading Partners.org (25 March 2024), Dario Toval wrote, "Literacy is broadly defined as the oppressed ability to read and write....Restricting access to literacy education for certain groups has a long-standing place in U.S. history, especially as a tool to purposely disrupt and damage the Black community and deny them their guaranteed and protected freedoms, liberties and rights in American life." In "Close Reading and Critical Theory" (2018) All NMU Master's Theses: 541, Kimberly L. Rosewall wrote "The act of close reading, the very foundation of literary study, is defined by Elaine Showalter in "Teaching Literature" (Wiley-Blackwell: 2002), as "an attentive, repetitive, and slow reading of a text with a deliberate attempt to detach and to pay close attention to language inside the text and close attention to factors outside the text."

For example, in terms of his formal and informal education, Howard Thurman wrote in "With Head and Heart: The Autobiography of Howard Thurman" (Harcourt Brace Jovanovich: 1979), "Had it not been for Benjamin Mays, for example, it is doubtful that I would have journeyed North to Columbia University in New York City to take the course on formal philosophy, mays awakened in me a keen interest in philosophy." In "With Head and Heart: The Autobiography of Howard Thurman" (Harcourt Brace Jovanovich: 1979), Howard Thurman wrote, "At that time, Morehouse offered a course in logic and a course in ethics, neither of which were strictly in the field, and no courses whatever in formal philosophy. I do not think that this was accidental. In the missionary colleges of the South, few (if any) courses were offered in the formal study of philosophy. I believe that the shapers of our minds, with clear but limited insight in the nature of our struggle for survival and development in American life, particularly in the South, recognized the real possibility that to be disciplined in the origin and development of ideas would ultimately bring under critical judgment the society and our position in it. This, in turn, would contribute to our unease and restlessness, which would be disastrous, they felt, for us and for our people. By the end of my sophomore year, I was determined to take such a course wherever I could find a college that would admit me for summer school."

In terms of his formal and informal education, Howard Thurman wrote in "The Search for Common Ground" (Friends United Press: 1971/1985), "All the dualisms of good and evil in one's life as a creature must exhaust themselves in a corroborating unity fundamental to the life process...." In "With Head and Heart: The Autobiography of Howard Thurman" (Harcourt Brace Jovanovich: 1979), "My testimony is that life is against all dualism...Life is One."

For example, Howard Robinson wrote in "Dualism" in "The Stanford Encyclopedia of Philosophy" (Spring 2023), "The term 'dualism' has a variety of uses in the history of thought. In general, the idea is that, for some particular domain, there are two fundamental kinds or categories of things or principles. In theology, for example a 'dualist' is someone who believes that Good and Evil – or God and the Devil – are independent and more or less equal forces in the world. Dualism contrasts with monism, which is the theory that there is only one fundamental kind, category of thing or principle; and, rather less commonly, with pluralism, which is the view that there are many kinds or categories. In the philosophy of mind, dualism is the theory that the mental and the physical – or mind and body or mind and brain – are, in some sense, radically different kinds of things."

In addition, in "A Look at Cartesian Dualism" Univ. of Pennsylvsina. edu (n.d.), John Alison wrote, "Dualism is the claim that there are two, essentially different kinds or types of objects or categories in the world. In the setting of a dualistic theory all objects that exist, or can exist, in the ontology of the world, fall under one of the two categories. The two forms of reality are said to be essential different because they are mutually exclusive and are often defined by opposite characteristics." In "A Look at Cartesian Dualism" Univ. of Pennsylvsina.edu (n.d.), John Alison wrote, "Although these two states of existence are fundamentally different in most ways, both are needed to give a complete description of reality. Perhaps the best and most apparent example of dualism is that which Descartes is led to through his metaphysical investigations in his "Meditations." One of the conclusions reached by Descartes in the Meditations is that all entities that exist in the world fall under one of two categories, minds or bodies. Minds, according to Descartes, are intangible, un-extended, and metaphysically prior to bodies. They are thinking things, entities capable of affirming, denying, judging, willing, unwilling, and having sense perceptions. Bodies on the other hand are tangible physical objects in the external world, have extension, and in some senses are seen to be reliant on minds for their existence. In Descartes' philosophy we can see the characteristic signature of dualism. The entire universe is composed only of things falling into one of two categories. Everything is either a mind or a body, with no room for overlap. The essential features defining the two categories of substances are opposites, extension and tangibility of bodies on the one hand and non-extension and intangibility of minds on the other. And lastly, we find the need for both types of reality. The world cannot be cast."

Moreover, Kevin Prchal wrote in "Light and Dark: The Duality of Good and Evil" Essai (01 April 2012) "[Dualism as] stories of good versus evil have been written and told for as long as history can remember....No story of good versus evil can surpass what some believe to be the origins of this ongoing theme in our lives; the story of God and Lucifer. Lucifer was a perfect angel, created by the vision of God. His appearance was radiant and beautiful, and he was crowned the Chief Covering angel in the kingdom of Heaven. As the Chief Covering angel, Lucifer spent much of his time with God the father and Jesus Christ. However, after some time, Lucifer started to become jealous of God's relationship with Jesus, and he set out to prove that he was above Jesus. In this campaign, he rallied the support of nearly one third of the angels in heaven, all of whom started to worship Lucifer instead of Jesus. God urged Lucifer and his army to end this behavior, but it only got worse, and God was forced to throw Lucifer out of heaven, along with his misguided followers. Some believe that ever since Lucifer was thrown from the gates of heaven, he has been taking shape in many different ways on earth, corrupting the image of life that God intended for us."

Todd Calder wrote in "The Concept of Evil," in "The Stanford Encyclopedia of Philosophy" (Winter 2022), "....it is important to note that there are at least two concepts of evil: a broad concept and a narrow concept. The broad concept picks out any bad state of affairs, wrongful action, or character flaw. The suffering of a toothache is evil in the broad sense as is a harmless lie. Evil in the broad sense has been divided into two categories: natural evil and moral evil. Natural evils are bad states of affairs which do not result from the intentions or negligence of moral agents. Hurricanes and toothaches are examples of natural evils. By contrast, moral evils do result from the intentions or negligence of moral agents. Murder and lying are examples of moral evils."   Todd Calder wrote in "The Concept of Evil," in "The Stanford Encyclopedia of Philosophy" (Winter 2022), "Evil in the broad sense, which includes all natural and moral evils, tends to be the sort of evil referenced in theological contexts, such as in discussions of the problem of evil. The problem of evil is the problem of accounting for evil in a world created by an all-powerful, all-knowing, all-good God. It seems that if the creator has these attributes, there would be no evil in the world. But there is evil in the world. Thus, there is reason to believe that an all-powerful, all-knowing, all-good creator does not exist."

Moreover, Todd Calder wrote in "The Concept of Evil," in "The Stanford Encyclopedia of Philosophy" (Winter 2022), "In contrast to the broad concept of evil, the narrow concept of evil picks out only the most morally despicable sorts of actions, characters, events, etc. As Marcus Singer puts it in The Concept of Evil," Philosophy (1979), , "'evil' [in this sense] … is the worst possible term of opprobrium imaginable."

In terms of his formal and informal education, in "Mysticism and Social Change" (Peter Lang Vertag; 1928), Howard Thurman wrote, "We must be thinkers and must learn how to think." Similarly, Donella H. Meadows et al, wrote in "The Limits to Growth" (Universe Books: 1972), "Of all the ways to produce social change the one with the most leverage is not tax incentives, spending austerity, nor the accumulation of wealth. Of all the ways to produce social change, the one with the most leverage is a change in how we think..." In "Hannah Arendt on Thinking" in "Cambridge Companion to Hannah Arendt" (Cambridge Univ.

Press: 2000/2002), edited by Dana Villa, Hannah Arendt remarked in "Hannah Arendt on Thinking" in "Cambridge Companion to Hannah Arendt" (Cambridge Univ. Press: 2000/2002), edited by Dana Villa, "There are no dangerous thoughts; thinking itself is dangerous." Martin Heidegger wrote in "What Is Called Thinking" (Perennial: 1954/2001), translated by J. Glen Gary, "We are trying to learn thinking.... thinking is thinking only when it pursues whatever speaks "for" a subject. We must learn thinking because our ability to think is still no guarantee that we are capable of thinking. Even so, it remains strange. And it seems presumptuous to assert that what is most thought-provoking in our thought-provoking time is that we are still not thinking...."

Moreover, Howard Thurman wrote in "Mysticism and Social Change" (Beacon Press: 1928), "We must make every major field of knowledge our province." For instance, Bruce Janz wrote in "Julie Klein, "Interdisciplinarity: History, Theory and Practice" (Wayne State Press: 1990), "Interdisciplinarity prompts a "unity of method," and as "unity of pragmatic application," and ability to dialogue freely across previously guarded disciplinary borders...." In "Critical Thinking" 8th Annual International Conference on Critical Thinking and Education Reform, Summer (1987), Nakato Hirakubo wrote, "'Synthesis' is to creatively or divergently apply prior knowledge and skills to produce a new or original whole: appraise, argue, arrange, assemble, categorize, collect, combine, compile, compose, construct, create, defend, design, develop, devise, evaluate, explain, formulate, generate, imagine, invent, judge, manage, modify, organize, plan, predict, prepare, propose, rearrange, reconstruct, relate, reorganize, revise, rewrite, select, set up, summarize, support, tell, value, write." Conor Detwiler observes that "A close and connected observation of nature reveals something more like a Celtic knot: a form without end or beginning. Not a system, but a synthesis."

Julie Thompson Klien wrote in "Interdisciplinarity" (Wayne State Univ. Press: 1990), "There is a subtle restructuring of knowledge in the late twentieth century. New divisions of intellectual labor increased borrowing across disciplines and a variety of "unified" "holistic" perspectives have created pressures upon traditional divisions of knowledge." In "Crossing Boundaries: Knowledge, Disciplinarity, and Interdisciplinarity "(Univ. Press of Virginia: 1996) Julie Thompson Klien wrote, "The long-term structural trends of academic institutions have been in the direction of greater specialization, professionalization, departmentalization, and fragmentation. Yet, cross-fertilization, overlaps and exchanges are proliferating...." In addition, Julie Thompson Klien wrote in "Crossing Boundaries: Knowledge, Disciplinarity, and Interdisciplinarity" (Univ. Press of Virginia: 1996), "There is a subtle restructuring of knowledge in the late twentieth century. New divisions of intellectual labor increased borrowing across disciplines and a variety of "unified" "holistic" perspectives have created pressures upon traditional divisions of knowledge..." Moreover, Julie Thompson Klien wrote in "Crossing Boundaries: Knowledge, Disciplinarity, and Interdisciplinarity" (Univ. Press of Virginia: 1996), "Holism and interdisciplinarity share a common interest of questioning the boundaries of genre, discourse, discipline, practice and theory.... All interdisciplinary work is critical in that it exposes the inadequacies of the existing organization of knowledge...."

In terms of his formal and informal education,   in "With Head and Heart: The Autobiography of Howard Thurman" (Mariner: 1979/1981), Howard Thurman wrote, "I majored in economics. But I could not consider myself educated until I was able to predict the effect of modes of production and consumption upon my life as a Black man in America."

Bob Jessup wrote in "Modes of Production" (Macmillan: 1990), edited by J. Entwell, et al, "Karl Marx used the concept of the ownership of the modes of production and consumption in two main ways; to analyze the economic base and to describe the overall structure of societies. Thus, he employed it to specify the particular combination of forces and relations of production which distinguished one form of labor process and its corresponding form of economic exploitation from another. He also employed it to characterize the overall pattern of social reproduction arising from the relations between the economic base (comprising production, exchange, distribution and consumption) and the legal, political, social and ideological institutions of the so-called superstructure."

In terms of his formal and informal education, Howard Thurman wrote in "Jesus and the Disinherited" (Beacon Press: 1949), "The underprivileged oppressed in any society are victims of perpetual war of nerves. The logic of the state of affairs is violence inflicted upon members of oppressed minority groups in American society." For example, Lukas Vartiak et al wrote in "Logic as a Tool for Developing Critical Thinking"

Rupkatha Journal (02 Nov 2023), "The starting point for developing critical thinking skills should be logic. Logic as a science of correct thinking is the basis on which the program for developing critical thinking is based." "Logic as a Tool for Developing Critical Thinking" Rupkatha Journal (02 Nov 2023), Lukas Vartiak et al wrote, "The connection between critical thinking and the skill of logical analysis can be traced almost throughout the history of the development of philosophical thinking. Prototypes of the term's modern connotations can be found in Socrates' famous method of constant and continuous questioning."

Jaakko J. Hintikka wrote in "Logic" Encyclopedia Britannica (07 June 2025), "Logic is the study of correct reasoning, especially as it involves the drawing of inferences." Jaakko J. Hintikka wrote in "Logic" Encyclopedia Britannica (07 June 2025), "An inference   is a rule-governed step from one or more propositions, called premises, to a new proposition, usually called the conclusion. A rule of inference is said to be truth-preserving if the conclusion derived from the application of the rule is true whenever the premises are true. Inferences based on truth-preserving rules are called deductive, and the study of such inferences is known as deductive logic. An inference rule is said to be valid, or deductively valid, if it is necessarily truth-preserving. That is, in any conceivable case in which the premises are true, the conclusion yielded by the inference rule will also be true. Inferences based on valid inference rules are also said to be valid."

Howard Thurman wrote in "With Head and Heart: The Autobiography of Howard Thurman" (Harcourt Brace Jovanovich: 1979), "We were citizens in the classical Greek sense of the concept, concerned with all aspects of the welfare of the State, responsible but penetrating critics aiding in every effort to make the good life possible for all people." For example, John Locke remarked, "The purpose of education is to enable individuals to think critically." James Baldwin remarked, "I love America more than any other country in the world and, exactly for this reason, I insist on the right to criticize her perpetually." Sverre Raffnsøe wrote in "What is Critique?" Critical Practice Studies (2017), "Modern, Western democracies have often defined themselves in distinction from totalitarianism, because critique is possible in this setting, but also because critique is a core task and makes up an important commitment. The willingness to subject other views to critical thinking is not only assumed in political systems and public debate. The possibility of critique and commitment to criticism is installed as an essential component in many societal institutions...."

David M. Johnson wrote in "Critique of Fascism" Virginia Commonwealth University.edu (n.d.), "Observation suggests that fascism is part of and similar to all the other "isms" that plague the world today. These "isms" include racism (the oppression of groups supposedly based on so-called " racial characteristics" and sexism (the oppression of females by mates). These "isms," including colonialism, imperialism, and fascism, all relate to the systematic oppression of some groups by others, and their presence and practice is almost universal.... The widespread influence of empires and the overlap between different ideologies make it difficult to pinpoint which ideology is responsible for specific forms of repression."

In "Critical Thinking" in The Stanford Encyclopedia of Philosophy (Summer 2024), David Hitchcock wrote in "Critical thinking is a widely accepted educational goal use of the term 'critical thinking' to describe an educational goal goes back to the American philosopher John Dewey in "How We Think" (D.C. Heath: 1910), who more commonly called it 'reflective thinking'. He defined it as "active, persistent and careful consideration of any belief or supposed form of knowledge in the light of the grounds that support it, and the further conclusions to which it tends" and identified a habit of such consideration with a scientific attitude of mind. His lengthy quotations of Francis Bacon, John Locke, and John Stuart Mill indicate that he was not the first person to propose development of a scientific attitude of mind as an educational goal...." David Hitchcock wrote in "Critical Thinking" in The Stanford Encyclopedia of Philosophy (Summer 2024), "What is critical thinking? Following John Rawls in "A Theory of Justice" (Harvard Univ. Press: 1971), who distinguished his conception of justice a characteristic set of principles for assigning basic rights and duties and for determining... the proper distribution of the benefits and burdens of social cooperation for the oppressed."

Further, D. Alan Bensley wrote in "Critical Thinking, Intelligence, and Unsubstantiated Beliefs: An Integrative Review" Journal of Intelligence (17 Oct 2023), "A review of the research shows that critical thinking is a more inclusive construct than intelligence, going beyond what general cognitive ability can account for. For instance, critical thinking can more completely account for many everyday outcomes, such as how thinkers reject false conspiracy theories, paranormal and pseudoscientific claims, psychological misconceptions, and other unsubstantiated claims. Deficiencies in the components of critical thinking (in specific reasoning skills, dispositions, and relevant knowledge) contribute to unsubstantiated belief endorsement in ways that go beyond what standardized intelligence tests test. Specifically, people who endorse unsubstantiated claims tend to show better critical thinking skills, possess more relevant knowledge, and are more disposed to thinking critically. They tend to be more scientifically skeptical and possess a more rational–analytic cognitive style, while those who accept unsubstantiated claims tend to be more cynical and adopt a more intuitive–experiential cognitive style."

Moreover, in "Critical Thinking and Critical Theory: An Exploration in Theory and Practice" (Routledge: 2008), Jennifer Moon wrote, "The concept, "critical," has several meanings. The most common meaning is to find fault, to judge, or to criticize. We use critical to refer to an intellectual skill of analysis as critical thinking, means to think with complexity; to go below the surface when considering a problem and explore its multiple dimensions and nuances and to think with complexity..." In addition, Jennifer Moon wrote in "Critical Thinking and Critical Theory: An Exploration in Theory and Practice" (Routledge: 2008), "Critical Theory" refers, as well, to a body of scholarship referred to as "Critical Theory." Critical Theory is a complex theoretical perspective, and mastery requires ongoing study and practice. Even a preliminary understanding of its principles can offer thinking tools for critical thinking about how American society works."

Maurice Waite wrote in "Paperback Oxford English Dictionary" (Oxford: 2012), "The concept, "problem," is defined as "something that is difficult to deal with and is difficult to understand in a society." Angus Stevenson wrote in "The Oxford Dictionary of English" (Oxford: 2010), "The concept, "problem," is variously defined as "dangers, debates, difficulties, dilemmas, disasters, disputes, disruptions, issues, problems, puzzles, questions, situations and tasks for which problems are not easily resolved and/or solved." Angus Stevenson wrote on "Oxford Dictionary of English" (Oxford: 2010), "The concepts, "reflect," "reflection," and "reflective," are derived from the Latin "pensare," which is variously defined as "to cogitate on, to contemplate, to deliberate about, to examine, to immerse in feelings, to inquire, to investigate, to meditate on, to mull over, to muse, to ponder, to question assumptions, to detach by suspending judgment, to reflect on, to review, to ruminate, to scrutinize, and to think about seriously."

For example, in terms of his formal and informal education and in contradiction to the problem discovery and problem solutions offered by countless social media platforms and countless podcasts, Howard Thuman wrote in "Temptations of Jesus" (Lawton Kennedy: 1962), "I read John Dewey's "How We Think" (D. C. Heath & Co: 1910). It examined a basic methodological approach to problem discovery and problem solving in all fields of investigation, from simple decision-making, to understanding and the treatment of disease and the most confused patterns of human action, activity, and behavior. It defined and described the process of reflective thinking as problem discovery and problem solving. First, the problem must be felt. Then, the problem must be defined and described as precisely as possible."

In "With Head and Heart: The Autobiography of Howard Thurman" (Harcourt Brace & Company: 1979), Howard Thurman wrote "During a 1922 in-residence summer course in the philosophy of government and in the philosophy of reflective thinking at Columbia University, in New York City, we used the text, Columbia University Associate's in Philosophy, "Introduction to Reflective Thinking" (Houghton Mifflin: 1923). It examined a basic methodological approach to problem solving in all fields of investigation, from simple decision-making, to understanding and the treatment of disease and the most confused patterns of human action, activity, and behavior. The course established for me a basic approach that I would use not only in my counseling, such as counseling leaders as we all as counseling student-leaders and children in the Civil Rights Movement, but also in thinking through the complex and complicated problems I would encounter in my personal life and as a social being. As a tool of the mind, there is no way by which the value of this course can be measured or assessed."

John Dewey wrote in "John Dewey: The Later Works, 1925-1953" (Southern Illinois University Press: 1984), edited by Jo Ann Boydston, "It is a familiar and significant saying that a problem half-understood is a problem half-solved. Yet, intellectualization of the difficulty or perplexity has to be felt into a problem in order to be solved." Laurence L. Buermeyer wrote in "Introduction to Reflective Thinking" (Houghton Mifflin: 1923), "When thinking is bent on solving a problem, on finding out the meaning of a perplexing situation, or reaching a conclusion that is worthy of belief, confidence, and faith, reflective to be distinguished from other kinds of thinking." Dr. Neha Jha and Mittal Shah wrote "Reflective Thinking: An Insight" IJRAR (2018),"John Dewey wrote in "How We Think: A Restatement of the Relation of Reflective Thinking to the Educative Process" (D.C. Heath & Co.: 1933), "The process of reflective thinking is an active, persistent and careful consideration of a belief or supposed form of knowledge, on grounds that justify and support that knowledge and further conclusions to which that knowledge leads. Reflective thinking and critical thinking are found to be used interchangeably at many places. The two concepts, reflective thinking and critical thinking are critical." In "Investigating Insight as Sudden Learning" The Journal of Problem Solving (Spring 2012), Ivan K. Ash, et al wrote, "Based on.... definitions one can see common themes underlying the concept of "insight" such as suddenness, restructuring/reorientation, and difficulty/fixation. In these examples, the term insight is used in very different ways. In one definition, insight is a psychological experience or phenomenon. In the next, it is a particular problem-solving sequence. In the next, it is a type of problem situation. And, in the last example, insight is defined as a problem-solving process."

Karl Popper wrote in "The Logic of Scientific Discovery" (Routledge: 1935/2002), "A scientist engaged in a piece of research, say in physics, can attack his problem straight away the philosopher finds himself in a different position. He does not face an organized structure, but rather something resembling a heap of ruins; and he must first clear a space in which to begin to build." difficult to solve or settle, a doubtful case, or a complex task involving doubt and uncertainty...." Norman Seel wrote in "Problems: Definition, Types, and Evidence" In "Encyclopedia of the Sciences of Learning" (Springer: 2012), edited by Norman Seel, "A distinction can be made between "task" and "problem." Generally, a "task" is a well-defined piece of work that is usually imposed by another person and may be burdensome. A "problem" is generally considered to be a task, a situation, or person which is difficult to deal with or control due to complexity and intransparency. In everyday language, a problem is a question proposed for solution, a matter stated for examination or proof. In each case, a problem is considered to be a matter which is difficult to solve or settle, a doubtful case, or a complex task involving doubt and uncertainty in American society." Further, David A. Rochefort and Roger W. Cobb wrote in "Problem Definition," in "The Politics of Problem Definition" (Univ. Press of Kansas: 1994), edited by David A. Rochefort and Roger W. Cobb, "As political discourse, the function of problem definition is at once, to describe, to explain, to recommend, and, above all, to persuade all to persuade."

Angus Stevenson wrote in "The Oxford Dictionary of English" (Oxford: 2010), "The concept, "complexity," is defined as "a condition, a quality, and a state of being and existing as complicated, composite, interconnected, interdependent, interrelated, intersectional, intricate, multi-dimensional, multi-faceted and variegated." Maurice Waite wrote in "Paperback Oxford English Dictionary" (Oxford: 2012), "The concepts, "complex" and "complexity," are defined as "difficult and hard to understand because of consisting of complicated and inseparable, interconnected, interdependent, and interrelated components, fragments, and parts." In addition, Julie Creswell wrote "Oxford Dictionary of Word Origins" (Oxford: 2010), that "The word "system," comes to us via Latin from Greek "sustema," of which the base elements are "sun" with and "histanai", "set up.""

In terms of his formal and informal education, Howard Thurman wrote in "The Search for Common Ground" (Friends United Press: 1971/1986). "The oppressed as living organisms consist of complex and" In "The Search for Common Ground" (Harper & Row: 1971), Howard Thurman wrote, "Mutual interdependence is characteristic of all life. And life is constructed of interconnected, interdependent, interrelated and intersectional systems within systems within systems." On the other hand, Howard Thurman wrote in "The Growing Edge" (Harper &Brothers: 1956), "There is ever the temptation to reduce all problems to a single problem, and to seize upon a single explanation for all the ills of life. Yet, like life itself, human beings are complex."

For instance, Ross D. Arnold and Jon P. Wade wrote in "A Definition of Systems Thinking: A Systems Approach" Science Direct (2015), "This paper proposes a definition of systems thinking for use in a wide variety of disciplines, with particular emphasis on the development and assessment of systems thinking educational efforts.....Many different definitions of systems thinking can be found throughout the systems community, but key components of a singular definition can be distilled from the literature.....Systems thinking is widely believed to be critical in handling the complexity facing the world in the coming decades...." Pearl Zhu wrote in "Systems Thinking Integrates Analysis and Synthesis" in "Understanding and Thinking Brigita Misiunaite et al wrote in "Can Holistic Education Solve the World's Problems: A Systematic Literature Review" Sustainability (2022), "Systems Thinking integrates analysis and synthesis."

James Ladyman and Karoline Wiesnar wrote in "What is a Complex System?" (Yale Univ Press: 2020), "It is important to understand complex systems because they are everywhere." Laying bare the fundamental mechanisms of the nature of power and oppression." In addition, James Ladyman and Karoline Wiesnar wrote in "What is a Complex System?" (Yale Univ Press: 2020), "Complexity, is a scientific theory which asserts that some systems of power display behavioral phenomena that are completely inexplicable by any conventional analysis of the systems' constituent parts. These phenomena, commonly referred to as emergent behavior, seem to occur in many complex systems involving living organisms...." In "What is a Complex System?" (Yale Univ Press: 2020), James Ladyman and Karoline Wiesnar wrote, "Complex networks of power can represent vastly different types of systems and the connections in a network of power may represent interactions of various kinds."

In "What is Complexity?" Digital Life Laboratory (2002), Christoph Adami wrote, "In dynamical systems theory, we are interested in the complexity of processes. For example, periodic and random processes are both perceived as simple, with the random processes at "the other end of the scale, whatever that scale may be. Complex and chaotic processes are deemed to lie somewhere in between. This ordering along a scale supports the general idea of a relationship between structure and complexity, as the consensus is that neither periodic nor random processes possess any structure in American society." Murray Gell-Mann wrote in "What Is Complexity?" Complexity (Wiley: 1995), "Any complex adaptive system can, of course, make mistakes in spotting regularities. We human beings, who are prone to superstition and often engage in denial of the obvious, are all too familiar with such errors.....Yet, any entity in the world around us, such as an individual human being, owes its existence not only to the simple fundamental law of physics and the boundary condition on the early universe but also to the outcomes of an inconceivably long sequence of probabilistic events, each of which could have turned out differently."

Murray Gell-Mann wrote in "What Is Complexity?" (Wiley: 1995), "As the universe grows older and frozen accidents pile up, the opportunities for effective complexity to increase keep accumulating as well. Thus, there is a tendency for the envelope of complexity to expand even though any given entity may either increase or decrease its complexity during a given time period." In "What Is Complexity?" (Wiley: 1995), Murray Gell-Mann wrote, "The appearance of more and more complex forms is not a phenomenon restricted to the evolution of complex adaptive systems, although for those systems the possibility arises of a selective advantage being associated under certain circumstances with increased complexity. The second law of thermodynamics, which requires average entropy (or disorder) to increase, does not in any way forbid local order from arising through various mechanisms of self-organization, which can turn accidents into frozen ones producing extensive regularities. Again, such mechanisms are not restricted to complex adaptive systems."

In terms of his formal and informal education, Howard Thurman wrote in "Deep is the Hunger: Meditation for Apostles of Sensitiveness" (Friends United Press: 1956/1986), "....even when we have done our best thinking, the most honest probing of our own motives, plumbed the depth of our innermost accumulative experience of living, we may arrive at a conclusion less than right....It is a simple but terrible truth that, in the most fundamental decisions we make, we must act on the basis of evidence and facts that are not quite conclusive."

Further, on the one hand, Howard Thurman wrote in "The Search for Common Ground" (Harper & Row: 1971), "Any analysis may need evidence and facts as explanation for actions, activities, behavior, conduct and events which explains why." In "Jesus and the Disinherited" (Beacon Press: 1949), Howard Thurman wrote, "When we undertake to do character analysis, uniqueness always tends to escape us." On the other hand, Howard Thurman wrote in "Jesus and the Disinherited" (Beacon Press: 1949), "White supremacists have always sought justification for indulging in all of their anti-colored assumptions, attitudes and beliefs."

For example, Ali Hassan wrote in "The Structure of Justification" in "The Blackwell Companion to Epistemology" (Blackwell: 1992/2010), "You probably agree with me that at least some of our beliefs are justified....You probably also agree that many of these beliefs depend for their justification on other beliefs......any justified belief must either be a basic, non-inferentially justified belief or, if it is non-basic, it must depend for its justification on other beliefs which must themselves be justified, with this regress of justification terminating, sooner or later, with basic beliefs." Ali Hassan wrote in "The Structure of Justification" in "The Blackwell Companion to Epistemology" (Blackwell: 1992/2010), "We should distinguish conceptually between three importantly different senses of "foundational belief": (i) a belief that does not depend for its justification on any other beliefs, (ii) a belief that does not depend for its justification on one's "justification" for any other beliefs, and (iii) a belief that does not depend for its justification on its "inferential relation" to other beliefs. At the same time, it should not be surprising that much of the focus of the debate in the literature is with (broadly) inferential vs. non-inferential justification, for a great many of our beliefs seem to be justified by their inferential (deductive, inductive, or explanatory) relations with other beliefs."

Further, Michael Beaney and Thomas Raysmith wrote in "Analysis" in "The Stanford Encyclopedia of Philosophy" (Fall 2024), "Analysis has always been at the heart of philosophical method, but it has been understood and practiced in many ways. Perhaps, in its broadest sense, it might be defined as a process of identifying or working back to what is more fundamental by means of which something, initially taken as given, can be derived, explained, or reconstructed. The derivation, explanation, or reconstruction is sometimes conceived as the corresponding process of synthesis, but it is more often counted as part of the analytic project as a whole. This allows great variation in specific methods, however. The aim may be to get back to basics and elucidate connections, but there may be all sorts of ways of doing this, each of which might be called 'analysis'." Kevin Mulligan and Fabrice Correia wrote in "Facts," in "The Stanford Encyclopedia of Philosophy" (Winter 2021), "The concept, "fact," is used in at least two different ways. In the locution "matters of fact," facts are taken to be what is contingently the case, or that of which we may have empirical or a posteriori knowledge. Thus, David Hume famously wrote at the beginning of Section IV of "An Enquiry concerning Human Understanding" (Clarendon Press; 1748), "All the objects of human reason or inquiry may naturally be divided into two kinds, to wit, Relations of Ideas and Matters of Fact.""

In "Facts," in "The Stanford Encyclopedia of Philosophy" (Winter 2021), Kevin Mulligan and Fabrice Correia wrote, "The word "fact", particularly when it is understood in the functorial sense, belongs to a family of related terms: "context," "circumstance", "situation (Sachlage)", "state of affairs (Sachverhalt)......" In "The Legal Concept of Evidence" in "The Stanford Encyclopedia of Philosophy" (Winter 2021), Hock Lai Ho wrote in Evidence.....is divided conventionally into three main categories: oral evidence (the testimony given in court by witnesses), documentary evidence (recorded and/or written documents produced for inspection by the court), and "real evidence"; the first two are self-explanatory and the third captures things other than recorded and/or written documents of resistance to oppression in American society." In addition, in "The Stanford Encyclopedia of Philosophy" (Winter 2021), Hock Lai Ho wrote. "......evidence of resistance is interconnected, interdependent, intersectional and thus is relational......and can serve drawing inferences (directly or indirectly) to a matter that is material to the case of Black resistance to oppression in American life." In, "Philosophical Perspectives 2, Epistemology" (Ridgeview: 1988), edited by James Tomberlin, Jaegwon Kim wrote, "The concept of evidence of resistance is inseparable from that of justification for beliefs, action, activity, behavior, conduct and events of resistance.... one thing is 'evidence' for another just in case the first tends to enhance the reasonableness or justification of the second.... A strictly non normative concept of evidence is not our concept of evidence; it is something that we do not understand...."

Moreover, Lyman R. Patterson wrote in "The Types of Evidence" Vanderbilt Law Review (Dec 1965), "Analysis is a process the purpose of which is to determine the relationship of the parts of a whole so as to ascertain the purpose, function, and nature of resistance. With respect to evidence, the process is one of determining the relationship of the parts which constitute the evidence to the proposed conclusion. This is because evidence is a relative term; evidence of resistance in order to be evidence, must be related to a proposed conclusion of Black resistance..." In "The Types of Evidence" Vanderbilt Law Review (Dec 1965), Lyman R. Patterson wrote, "Evidence of resistance is a term ordinarily used to indicate facts which produce conviction in the mind as to the existence of another fact of resistance."

Furthermore, Mohammad Firoz Khan wrote in "What Is Reality? What Are Facts?" Research Gate (22 Jan 2014), "Facts are statements about some events or circumstances that exist or that have occurred. Facts are observable (measurable), verifiable and indisputable whatever measure of reason and logic is applied to or reject them reality is not simply acknowledged but must be discovered or reasoned and is liable to falsification." On the other hand, Naomi Oreskes wrote in "Why Trust Science?" (Princeton Univ. Press: 2021), "Facts are "hardened" through persuasion and their use......hardening, persuasion and use of facts occurs via experience and observation of the natural world; another is the critical of claims based on those experiences and observations."

Maurice Waite wrote in "Paperback Oxford Dictionary" (Oxford 2012), "The concept, "empathy," is defined as "the action, activity, behavior and conduct of first feeling and then understanding the pain of other human beings." On the one hand, Joe Rigney wrote in "The Sin of Empathy" (Canon Press: 2025), "The so-called virtue of empathy is the greatest rhetorical tool of manipulation in the 21st century." Yet, Karen Garcia wrote in "What It Means To Be An Empath" Los Angeles Times (04 April 2023), "identifying as an empath takes the sensitivity aspect of feeling an outsider's pain to another level — an empath absorbs it."

On the other hand, in terms of his formal and informal education Howard Thurman wrote in "Deep is the Hunger: Meditations for Apostles of Sensitiveness" (Friends United Press: 1947/1986), "We were feeling creatures before we were thinking creatures. For "to feel is to do." In "With Head and Heart: The Autobiography of Howard Thurman" (Harcourt, Brace and Jovanovich: 1979), Howard Thurman wrote, "It is a misreading of the role of feelings to separate them from the function of the mind at work! No matter how clear and penetrating and detached the vast reaches of creative thoughts may be at their best, they are but lifeless forms until they are energized by the continuum of emotion that is always present and antedates the emergence of the mind. After all, it may be true that what is called "thought" is a function of feeling, reduced to slow motion." Further, Howard Thurman wrote in "Jesus and the Disinherited" (Beacon Press: 1949), Howard Thurman wrote, "It is a grievous blunder for the oppressed to think that all understanding of oppression will be empathetic." In "Meditations of the Heart" (Friends United Press: 1953/1986), Howard Thurman wrote, "For the oppressed, often there is a great relief to be able to put into words the quality or the very nuance of need, pain and suffering. For the oppressed, to suffer in dumb silence, to be able to find no word capable of voicing what is being experienced, seems degrading to the self because it pushes the individual back into a vast continuum from which he has emerged into a personality, self-conscious and self-aware...."

Leo Tolstoy wrote in "The Death of Ivan Ilyich and Other Stories" (Penguin: 1917/2008), "For the oppressed, to feel pain is to be alive. To feel the pain of the oppressed is to be a human being." Alfred Adler remarked, "Empathy is seeing and listening to the oppressed and feeling them with the heart." Murat Aydede wrote in "Pain," in "The Stanford Encyclopedia of Philosophy" (Spring 2019), "Pain is the most prominent member of a class of sensations known as bodily sensations…Bodily sensations are typically attributed to bodily locations and appear to have features such as volume, intensity, duration, and so on, that are ordinarily attributed to physical objects or quantities….." Murat Aydede wrote in "Pain," in "The Stanford Encyclopedia of Philosophy" (Spring 2019), "There are two main threads in the common-sense conception of pain that pull in opposite directions….The first thread treats pains as particulars spatially located in body regions, or more generally, as particular conditions of body parts that have spatiotemporal characteristics as well as features such as intensity (among others). This thread manifests itself in common ways of attributing pains to bodily locations, such as the following: (1) I have a sharp pain in the back of my right hand. (2) There is a throbbing pain in my left thigh. (3) My right shoulder hurts.(4) My wisdom tooth aches. According to this thread, pains are like physical objects or specific conditions of physical objects. We also commonly use the verbs 'feel' or 'experience' to describe our epistemic relation to pains attributed to body parts. Pain is the most prominent member of a class of sensations known as bodily pain."

In addition, in "Pain," in "The Stanford Encyclopedia of Philosophy" (Spring 2019),Murat Aydede wrote, "The second thread is pain as subjective experience. That pain is a subjective experience that seems to be a truism. Given our common-sense understanding of pain, this seems to be the more dominant thread: instead of treating pains as objects of perceptual experience, it treats them as experiences themselves. Indeed, it is this thread that the official scientific definition of 'pain' picks up and emphasizes, which was first formulated in 1979 by a committee organized by the International Association for the Study of Pain (IASP), and has been, since then, widely accepted by the scientific community and clinicians…. Pain is always subjective…It is unquestionably a sensation in a part or parts of the body, but it is also always unpleasant and therefore also an emotional experience."

On the other hand, Joanna Bourke wrote in "Pain Sensitivity" NIH. gov (29 March 2014) "Who is truly capable of experiencing pain? While certain persons are regarded as "truly hurting," other person's distress can be disparaged or not even registered as being "real pain." Such judgments have had major effects on regimes of pain-alleviation. Indeed, it took until the late twentieth century for the routine underestimation of the sufferings of certain oppressed groups of people to be deemed deviant, disreputable, scandalous and unseemly. Often the categorizations of the pain of the oppressed are contradictory. For instance, the humble status of workers and immigrants mean that they are said to be insensitive to noxious stimuli; the profound inferiority of these same persons mean that they are especially likely to respond with "exaggerated" sensitivity. How did we hold such positions simultaneously? Pain-assignation claimed to be based on natural hierarchical schemas, but the dualism of good and evil in the great Chain of Feeling is more fluid than it seems."

In "Disciplines of the Spirit" (Friends United Press: 1963), Howard Thurman wrote "When it comes to the oppressed, very glibly does we speak of words like "compassion, caring, concern, pity," and "sitting where they sit." But to be empathetic toward the oppressed in actual and concrete experience, is genuinely to be rocked to one's foundation." Karsten Stueber wrote in "Empathy," in The Stanford Encyclopedia of Philosophy (Summer 2019), "The concept of empathy is used to refer to a wide range of embodied, biological, contextualized, and empathetic approaches. environmental, holistic, neurological, physiological, and psychological capacities that are thought of as being central for constituting the oppressed as human beings and social creatures allowing us to know what the oppressed are thinking and feeling, to emotionally engage with them, to share their thoughts and feelings, and to care for the well–being of the oppressed in American life."

Benedict Spinoza wrote in "Writings on Political Philosophy" (Appleton, 1937), "When it comes to the oppressed, I have labored carefully, not to mock, lament, or execute human actions, but to understand them." Carl Rogers remarked "For the oppressed, the highest expression of empathy is accepting and non-judgmental." In addition, Edward Titchener wrote in "Lectures on the Experimental Psychology of Thought-Processes" (Macmillan, 1909), the "...empathy is the action, the activity and the behavior of first looking into and then feeling into the lives of the oppressed."

In "The Oxford Dictionary of English" (Oxford: 2020), Angus Stevenson wrote, "The concept, "pretend," is variously defined "to connive, to deceive, to feign, and to simulate knowing and understanding something." The "Merriam-Webster English Dictionary" defines the concept, "understand," as "to grasp the meaning of; to grasp the reasonableness of; to have thorough or technical acquaintance with or expertness in the practice of; to be thoroughly familiar with the character and propensities of; to accept as a fact or truth or regard as plausible without utter certainty; and to supply in thought as though expressed."

In terms of his formal and informal education, Howard Thurman wrote in "Meditations of the Heart" (Beacon Press: 1953/1999), "Very often we pretend to understand what we do not understand concerning oppression. This is because understanding both oppressions, and the oppressed takes time. In the realm of facts, one has to work hard and carefully weigh and sifting and test before one arrives at an understanding. This takes time as well. Moreover, there must be a "will" to understand both the oppressed and oppression." To be sure, Frantz Fanon wrote in "The Wretched of the Earth" (Grove Press: 1961/1963), "Everything can be explained to the people, on the single condition that you want them to understand." Harold Cruse remarked, "I have often said......we have, for the most part, underestimated our situation in the United States.... We don't fully understand our situation in American society."

Stephen Grimm wrote in "The Concept of Understanding," in "The Stanford Encyclopedia of Philosophy" (Winter 2024), "Understanding resistance to oppression seems to be different than just mere knowledge about resistance to oppression in two respects. For one thing, understanding resistance typically seems harder to acquire, and more of an epistemic accomplishment than knowledge alone. For another, the object of understanding resistance to oppression seems more structured and interconnected. Thus, the subject matters of resistance to oppression we try to understand are often highly complex, dynamic, and fluid, especially when we try to understand isolated events of resistance. Nevertheless, we typically attempt to understand resistance to oppression by drawing connections with other events of Black resistance in American society." In "The Concept of Understanding," in "The Stanford Encyclopedia of Philosophy" (Winter 2024), Stephen Grimm wrote, "The goodness of an explanation of Black resistance to oppression therefore seems to have little obvious connection to whether it manages to generate understanding in a particular audience. A good explanation might be that. But then again, it might not. Patently poor explanations are also able to generate a rich "sense" of Black resistance to oppression in some audiences."

Again, in terms of his formal and informal education, in "Mysticism and Social Change" Lecture delivered during the Annual Convocation at Eden Theological Seminary in St. Louis (26 Feb 1928), Howard Thurman remarked, "When it comes to oppression, we must learn how to think and must make every major field of knowledge our province." For example, Keisuke Okamura wrote in "Interdisciplinarity Revisited" Palgrave Communications (2019), "Many of the contemporary problems of oppression are complex, interconnected, interdependent, interrelated, intersectional and therefore inseparable and cannot be addressed or resolved by any single academic discipline, requiring a multifaceted and integrated approach across academic disciplines." Julie Klein wrote in "A Conceptual Vocabulary of Interdisciplinary Science" in "Practicing Interdisciplinarity" (Univ. of Toronto Press: 2000), edited by P. Weingart and N. Stehr, "An intersection is a system of negotiating historical contexts."

In addition, Julie Klein wrote in "A Conceptual Vocabulary of Interdisciplinary Science" in "Practicing Interdisciplinarity" (Univ. of Toronto Press: 2000), edited by P. Weingart and N. Stehr, "All interdisciplinary work is critical in that it exposes the inadequacies of the existing organization of knowledge of academic specialists to accomplish given tasks of interpreting oppression as a complex, interconnected, interdependent, interrelated, intersectional and therefore inseparable historical contexts robust enough to maintain unity across academic fields."

The "Cambridge Dictionary of English" defines the concept, "pattern," "a definite, a particular and a specific way in which something is done, is "organized," or "happens." It has been remarked that "....in science, a pattern is a regular and repeatable arrangement or sequence that can be found in nature, in mathematics, or in other areas. Patterns are regular and intelligible forms or sequences that can be found throughout nature. Scientific questions may be generated when scientists observe a pattern of action, activity, behavior and events..."

In terms of his formal and informal education, Howard Thuman wrote in "The Search for Common Ground" (Harper & Row: 1971), "In the total panorama of the external world of nature there seems to a pattern of structural dependability and continuity, or what may be called an inner logic that manifests itself in forms and organizational schemes, and in a wide variety of time-space arrangements." Moreover, Howard Thurman wrote in "The Search for Common Ground" (Harper & Row: 1971), "The most striking pattern of all of this is that there seems to be an affinity between the human mind and all external forms, a fact that makes understanding of the world possible for the human mind."

Chuck Palahniuk remarked, "There are only patterns, patterns on top of patterns, patterns that affect other patterns. Patterns hidden by patterns. Patterns within patterns. If you look closely, history does nothing but repeat itself. What we call chaos is just patterns we haven't recognized. What we call random is just patterns we can't decipher. What we can't understand is nonsense. What we can't read we call gibberish. There is no free will. There are no variables." Christopher Alexander wrote in "A Pattern of Language" (Oxford: 1977/2018), "There is a myth, sometimes widespread, that the oppressed need only do inner work... that the oppressed are entirely responsible for their own problems; and that to cure themselves the oppressed need only change themselves." In "A Pattern of Language" (Oxford: 1977/2018), Christopher Alexander wrote, "A pattern describes a problem that occurs in our environment over and over again patterns are connected to other patterns...." Moreover, Christopher Alexander wrote in "A Pattern of Language" (Oxford: 1977/2018), "Rather than being accidental, arbitrary, random and/or unplanned, patterns are ordered and sequenced...."

In "A Pattern of Language" (Oxford: 1977/2018), Christopher Alexander wrote, "Patterns are interconnected, interdependent and interrelated because "....no pattern is an isolated entity. Each pattern can exist in the world, only to the extent that is supported by other patterns..." In "Thinking Fast and Slow" (Farrar, Straus and Giroux: 2011), Damiel Kahneman wrote, "We are pattern seekers, believers in a coherent world in which regularities and repetition not by accident but as a result of mechanical causality or of someone's conscious aim goal and intention." Further, Howard Margolis wrote in "Patterns, Thinking and Cognition: A Theory of Judgement" (Univ. of Chicago Press: 1987), "a pattern of actions, activities, behaviors, conduct and events is prompted by cues in the pattern of actions, activities, behaviors, conduct and events in context. The pattern itself then becomes part of the environment." In "Thinking in Patterns and the Pattern of Human Thought as Contrasted with AI Data Processing" Philosophy, Computer Science, Mathematics (08 April 2018), Robert K. Logan and Marlie Tandoc wrote, "Human beings both deal with information and engage in creative thinking, while computers only process data according to the instructions of their human programmers. We believe human beings are capable of both recognizing and creating patterns, but computers are only capable of recognizing the type of patterns that they have been programmed to look for. We believe computers are deduction engines that are also capable of induction, as is the case when they succeed at mastering chess or go. They are not capable of abductive reasoning or creating a story, however, and hence there are limits to their creativity."

In terms of his formal and informal education, Howard Thurman wrote in "The Search for Common Ground" (Harper & Row: 1971), "Since childhood I have always had a tendency for seeing whole which transcends all diversities in which diversity finds its richness and significance. For all human beings to be the same would mean the death of human beings. This is because mutual interconnectedness, mutual interdependence, mutual interrelatedness, and mutual intersectionality is characteristic of all life." On the other hand, Howard Thurman wrote in "The Search for Common Ground" (Harper: 1971), "Mutual interdependence is characteristic of all life. Therefore, the biosphere and the ecosphere, like all living organisms, are mutually interdependent systems within systems within systems." Howard Thurman also wrote in "Disciplines of the Spirit" (Friends United Press: 1963/1986), "There is an almighty synthesis that gives it an ultimate meaning and context."

Leonard F. Wheat in "Hegel's Undiscovered Thesis- Antithesis-Synthesis Dialectics" (Prometheus Books: 2012). "A "synthesis" is a result of putting together, assembling, or combining parts." Eileen McMillan, et al wrote in "Holism: A Concept Analysis" International Journal of Nursing & Clinical Practices (2018), "Holism loosely means including the whole being, mind, body, and soul, considering that something is more than a sum of the parts. Consequently, disturbance in one part of the whole system affects all the other parts of the system. One part cannot function without the whole." In "Can Holistic Education Solve the World's Problems: A Systematic Literature Review" Sustainability (2022). "Holistic learning theory is the theory upon which holistic education is based. These terms are used interchangeably in this chapter. There are many views on what holistic learning theory is or might be. This article provides an overview of some of the common elements. The solution to the evolution of education could be a holistic educational vision of education that connects a fragmented world, communities, societies, and individuals. However, what do we know about this educational paradigm? Holistic education is a new movement that emerged as a recognized field of study and practice in North America in the mid-1980s. In 1989, eighty education representatives signed the Chicago Statement. A year later, this agreement led to the publication of "Education 2000: A Holistic Perspective", which sets out ten principles for holistic education that fundamentally contradict the prevailing reductionist paradigm. A vision of holistic education based on ecological awareness, spirituality, relationships, and values was developed based on the work of Douglas Sloan, David Purcell, Ed Clark, Ron Miller, Phil Gang, Jack Miller, and Parker Palmer."

In terms of his formal and informal education, Howard Thurman wrote in "Deep is the Hunger: Meditations for Apostles of Sensitiveness" (Friends United Press: 1947/1986), "The tragedy of the modern liberal is the illusion that the ideal and the real, theory and practice can ever be separated from each other. Yet, practice and theory can never be separated from each other. This is because practice is theory realizing itself in concrete space and time..." In "What, for [Martin] Heidegger, was the Relationship between Practice and Theory" Academia.edu (n.d.)

William Parsons wrote, "For the purposes of this essay, 'practice' will be defined as our physical, practical actions, activities, behaviors, conduct and events in the world. Moreover, 'thinking' and 'thought' will be defined as embodied, holistic and organic and organic thinking. The relationship between thought and practice is essentially the relationship between human beings and the world around human beings."

Further, Xandra Eid wrote in "Idealism vs Realism" The Gazelle.org (18 Oct 2023), "......some have an ideal view of the world — an idealist perspective — and others see the real deal — a realist's perspective. A famous name associated with idealist thinking is Plato, also known as the father of idealism. At its core, idealism is the idea of scenarios of the world of oppression, which are not in the real world, but only in your mind. Realism is the unfiltered, per se, view of the life of oppression. Imagination is not so common with realists in comparison to idealists, where imagination is their understanding of the world that may tend to be how idealists view life." In "Beyond Dichotomies: Theory vs. Practice" at the Annual Meeting of the Comparative and International Education Society (CIES), Stanford University (March 22-26, 2005), Hans N. Weiler wrote, "theory" traditionally represents a kind of knowledge that is the generalized distillation of observations for the purpose of explaining other observations; its principal purpose lies in the constant perfection of its own explanatory power. Theoretical knowledge is rated by how well it explains as wide a range of phenomena as possible. "Practice", by contrast, is conventionally predicated on a more instrumental conception of knowledge; it represents knowledge that helps to accomplish things, and that proves its worth by how well it does help to accomplish whatever needs to be accomplished, and therefore by how closely it corresponds to the particulars of a given problem situation."

Angus Stevenson wrote in "Oxford Dictionary of English" (Oxford: 2010) "The concept, "dialectics," is the theory and practice of interrogating, probing, and questioning accepted, canonized, conventional and traditional ways of thinking in terms of abstractions, assumptions, beliefs, epistemologies, ethics, grand narratives, ideologies, judgments, moralities, myths, opinions, outlooks, philosophies, presumptions, universals, viewpoints and worldviews."" Julia Cresswell wrote in "The Oxford Dictionary of Word Origins" (Oxford 2010), "The concepts "contradict" and "contradiction," are defined as "the decree and the verdict of denying the reality of something in a society." In the "Oxford Dictionary of Difficult Words" (Oxford: 2004), Archie Hobson wrote. "The concepts "contradict," contradiction." "negate" and "negation," are defined as "the beliefs, ideologies, discourse, action, activity, behavior, conduct and events which deny the existence and the reality something."" In his "Paperback Oxford Dictionary" (Oxford: 2012), Maurice Waite wrote "The concept "contradiction," is a verb that means to deny the reality of something."

For example, Howard Thurman wrote in "The Search for Common Ground" (Harper & Row: 1971), "There are contradictions under which I must eke out my days as a member of the oppressed in American society." Moreover, in "Disciplines of the Spirit" (Friends United Press: 1963), Howard Thurman wrote, "The contradictions of life are never final. All contradictions are held together in an almighty synthesis that gives them ultimately, a meaning and a context." C.L.R. James wrote in "The Black Jacobins" (Penguin:1938/2011), "In terms of dialectics, the contradiction to reality as well as the negation of reality, is that there are and always will be some who, ashamed of the action, activity, behavior and conduct and of their ancestors, try to prove that the external and internal slave trade, the external and internal middle passages, chattel slavery, as well as post-Reconstruction physical terrorism and physical violence, was not so bad after all, that its evils, it's dangerous and deadly barbarism, its brutality and its cruelty were the exaggerations of propagandists and not the habitual lot of the slaves. Men will say (and accept) anything in order to foster national pride or soothe a troubled conscience."

In "Hegel's Dialectics" in "The Stanford Encyclopedia of Philosophy" (Winter 2020), Julie E. Maybee wrote "The concept, "dialectics," is a term used to describe a method and process of argument that involves contradictions and some of contradictory process between opposing sides the "dialectical" or "negatively rational" moment—is the moment of instability." Aristotle wrote in "Metaphysics" (Oxford: 1924), "A contradiction occurs when one observes the most certain of all logic which states that assertions which oppose each other are not simultaneously true is the firmest logic of all.... no one can believe that opposite assertions are one thing and are not at the same time... that the same thing can at the same time both belong and not belong to the same object and in the same respect."

Karl Marx and Friedrich Engels wrote in "The Collected Works" (u society (as a totality) in a critical way and connected normative questions directly with the analysis of social trends. By identifying the deep structures and driving mechanisms of historical developments, critique can thus glean characteristic forms of conflict and emancipatory possibilities from their constitutive tensions and "contradictions."" Further, in "A Pedagogy of Praxis: A Dialectical Philosophy of Education" (State University of New York Press: 1996), Moacir Gadotti wrote, "In ancient Greece, the word dialectic expressed a specific manner of argumentation which consisted of discovering the contradictions which were contained in the reasoning of the opponent, thus denying the validity of his argument and surpassing it by another synthesis." In "Critical Theory: Selected Essays" (Continuum: 1971), Max Horkheimer wrote, "The task of critical reflection is not merely to understand the contradictions of the evidence, the facts and the reality of oppression in their historical development, in American society." In addition, Theodore W. Adorno wrote in "Minima Moralia: Reflections from a Damaged Life" (Verso: 1944/2005). "A work must cut through the contradictions of power and oppression and overcome them, not by covering them up, but by pursuing them." In "Negative Dialectics" (Suhrkamp Verlag: 1966), Theodore W. Adorno wrote, "Thinking as such... is an act of negation and of resistance to that which is forced upon it; this is what thought has inherited from its archetype, the relation between labor and material related to the oppressed."

In "Culture, Dialectics and Reasoning About Contradiction." Univ of Mich.edu (n.d.), Kaiping Peng and Richard E. Nisbett wrote, "Dialectical thinking is considered to consist of sophisticated approaches towards seeming contradictions and inconsistencies. The key feature of Western dialectical thinking is integration, starting with the recognition of contradiction, then moving on to the reconciliation of basic elements of the opposing perspectives. Its rational foundation is still the law of non-contradiction, so that a satisfactory solution to contradiction is a non- contradictory one..." Moreover, Michael Basseches wrote in "Thinking, Reasoning, and Writing," edited by E. P. Maimon, et al (Longman Inc: 1989), "I view the dialectical perspective as comprising a family of world outlooks, or views of the nature of existence (ontology) and knowledge (epistemology), related to oppressed and the oppressed. These world outlooks, while differing from each other in many respects, share a family resemblance based on three features: common emphases on change, on wholeness, and on internal relations between the oppressed and American society." In "Valences of the Dialectic" (Verso: 2009/2020), Fredric Jamerson wrote, "Dialectics observes contradictions everywhere and always in American society." Laurence R. Horn who wrote in "Contradiction," in "The Stanford Encyclopedia of Philosophy" (Winter 2023), "The logical incoherence of contradictions is the ground for indecision."

Lawrence Wilde wrote in "Logic: Dialectic and Contradiction" Marxist.org (1991). "Dialectical philosophers claim that contradictions exist in reality and that the most appropriate way to understand the movement of that reality is to study the development of those contradictions. Formal logic denies that contradictions exist in reality, and where they are seen to exist in thought, they have to be expunged in order to arrive at the truth. This is embodied in the principle of non-contradiction, in which the presence of a contradiction in a statement or a proposition invalidates its claim to truth. On the face of it, therefore, the claims of dialectical and formal logic appear to be incommensurable, and dialogue between the two systems appears to be impossible. We must therefore look carefully at Marx's concept of contradiction and his scattered remarks on his own method..." In "Observations on the Education of Foreign Countries" (Forgotten Books: 2015/2018), Zhu Yongxin wrote, "When it comes to interpreting oppression and the lives of the oppressed in American society, the dialectical way of thinking is genuinely scientific." Finally, Bernice Yan and Patricia Arlin wrote in "Dialectical Thinking: Implications for Creative Thinking," Marc Runco and Steven Pritzer, Editors, "Encyclopedia of Creativity" (Academic Press: 1999), "An argument can be made that the overall process of dialectical thinking is in and of itself a creative process. One reason for the three-step dialectic formula (thesis-antithesis-synthesis) is designed like a feedback loop that would repeat itself endlessly. In this dialectical process, there is a constant opposition between creative change and the natural tendency to seek stability. This constant opposition creates a discomfort zone from which new and better ways of representing reality the reality of the oppressed continually emerge."

The "Merriam-Webster's Dictionary of English" defines "concept" as ?something conceived in the mind." In terms of his formal and informal education, Howard Thurman wrote in "The Search for Common

Ground" (Harper & Row: 1971), "Concepts in the mind are derivatives of one's experience with his senses." derivatives of one's experience with his senses." Harold Cruse wrote in "The Crisis of the Negro Intellectual" William Morrow & Co: 1967/1984). "The intellectual can, must, and will create concepts by which the oppressed can "struggle, live, and die for."" In addition, in "Black Rights/ White Wrongs" (Oxford: 2017), Charles W. Mills wrote, "concepts are necessary to apprehend, both in the empirical and moral realm." Charles W. Mills wrote "Black Rights/ White Wrongs" (Oxford: 2017). "Concepts drive perception, yet whites are aprioristically intent on denying the concepts before them." In "Concepts," in "The Stanford Encyclopedia of Philosophy" (Summer 2023), Eric Margolis and Stephen Laurence wrote, "Concepts are the building blocks of thinking and thought. Consequently, they are crucial to such biological, cognitive, neurological, physiological and psychological processes as categorization, inference, memory, learning, and decision-making, for critical theorists. This much is relatively uncontroversial. And concepts help to explain and to describe lived experiences."

Further, Peter Gärdenfors wrote in "From Sensations to Concepts" Review of Philosophy and Psychology (2019), "The senses and sensations are what is received by the senses. The learning process consists of the mechanism that utilizes primary domains for concept formation. There are strong arguments for that even the experience of\ space and in time must be learned through an "interaction" with the world of oppression around them in American society." I.C. Jarvie wrote in "Concepts and Society" (Routledge: 2014), "Robert Wortmann commented that, "The old Chinese proverb shows the importance of the senses in the learning process. The five senses of hearing, touch, sight, taste and smell are the primary means used to gain new knowledge. And we rarely experience one sense alone. The senses work together to give us a total picture of our experiences in American life." I.C. Jarvie wrote in "Concepts and Society" (Routledge: 2014). "There is a connection between thinking, feeling, thought, concepts, beliefs, ideas, ideologies and action, activity, and behavior, for critical theorists, and a connection between feeling, thinking, thought, concepts, beliefs, ideas, ideologies and action, activity, and behavior in any oppressive society."

John Blake wrote in "Are Whites Racially Oppressed?" CNN (04 March 2011), "They are, some say, the new face of racial oppression in this nation -- and their faces are white. A growing number of white Americans are acting like a racially oppressed majority. They are adopting the language and protest tactics of an embattled minority group, scholars and commentators say." Yet, on the one hand, Martin Luther King remarked, "The black revolution is much more than a struggle for the rights of Negroes. It is forcing America to face all its interrelated flaws— racism, poverty, militarism, and materialism. It is exposing evils that are rooted deeply in the whole structure of our society and suggests that radical reconstruction of society is the real issue to be faced...."

On the other hand, Captain Ibrahim Traore, President of Burkina Faso remarked, "The history of oppression isn't just about chains or laws. It is about the psychological weight that gets passed down...the quiet fear...the unspoken rules...the way you brace yourselves for rejection before it even happens. To every African in America feeling powerless, I want you to know that you are not alone. There's a reason you feel the weight pressing down on your shoulders. It is not imagined. It is real. It is generations deep. It is systems, silence, and survival woven together... Look around you. The struggle is shared....That feeling of being powerless, of being unheard, unseen, or pushed to the side, is not just in your mind. It's a heavy reality that many African persons in America carry silently every day. The weight isn't just from one bad moment or one bad experience. It is from years, decades, and centuries of being treated as less than human....of having your identity twisted, your dignity questioned, and your humanity ignored....Generations before you fought against this shared pain, some with words, some with their lives. And now you carry that same torch even when you don't realize it. You may feel tired. You may feel isolated. But even in those quiet moments of doubt you are not the only one fighting to hold on to dignity, to pride, to purpose...."

Howard Thurman wrote in "Jesus and the Disinherited" (Beacon Press: 1949) "The masses of the oppressed live with their backs constantly against the wall. The oppressed are the poor, the disenfranchised, the disinherited, the dispossessed and the exploited who are without protection for their persons in American society." For example, in "The First Duty of Government: Protection, Liberty and the Reconstruction Fourteenth Amendment" Duke University Law School (n.d.), Steven J. Heyman wrote, "As I shall argue, the congressional debates on the Reconstruction Fourteenth Amendment to the United States Constitution, proposed by the U.S. Congress on June 13, 1866 and ratified on July 9, 1868, show that establishing a federal constitutional right to protection of all persons was one of the central purposes of the Reconstruction Fourteenth Amendment to the United States Constitution. The principal aim of the Fourteenth Amendment was.... to incorporate into the Federal Constitution the fundamental freedoms, liberties and rights that Black lives already possess under general constitutional theory, but that the states had failed to enforce adequately."

In "Oppression and Power" Santa Clara Univeriry.edu (2019), G. L. Palmer wrote, "Oppression" is defined in "Merriam-Webster Dictionary" as: "Unjust or cruel exercise of authority or power especially by the imposition of burdens; the condition of being weighed down; an act of pressing down; a sense of heaviness or obstruction in the body or mind". This definition demonstrates the intensity of oppression, which also shows how difficult such a challenge is to address or eradicate. Further, the word oppression comes from the Latin root "primere," which actually means "pressed down". Importantly, we can conclude that oppression is the social act of placing severe restrictions on an individual, group, or institution. Moreover, oppression is often discussed in the same context as the terms "dehumanization" and "exploitation". These are terms that portray unjustness and cruelty upon the oppressed in a society." In Analyzing Oppression" (Oxford: 2006), Ann E. Cudd wrote, "More generally, the concept, "oppression" in the modern period refers to the arbitrary or unjust laws imposed on members of oppressed minority groups in American society."

Renita Seabrook and Heather Wyatt-Nichol wrote in "The Ugly Side of America: Institutional Oppression and Race" (2016). "Historical accounts of American institutions and hence institutional; structures and hence structural; systems and hence systemic oppression in the United States dates to Colonial Virginia. We contend that institutional, organizational, structural, and systemic oppression in American society today, is the result of institutional, organizational, structural and systemic oppression throughout American history." Further, Major Jeffrey Camlin wrote in "Defining the Oppressor" Philosophical Archive.org (06 Nov 2024), "An oppressor is defined as an entity that (1) possesses one or more of the four instruments of power—physical force, political power, economic power, or informational power—(2) is actively projecting its power directed at another individual, group, institution, or system, (3) the target of that power contains significantly less power than the projector, (4) is not a false accusation of oppression as revealed by a relative power comparison, and (5) restricts an individual or group's autonomy, limits access to resources or opportunities, or diminishes their social or cultural value."

Moreover, Serene J. Khader wrote in "Why Is Oppression Wrong?" Philos Studies (2024), "I suggest that oppression might be better thought of as an affront to guaranteed and protected freedoms, liberties and rights of the oppressed in a democratic society." In "Five Faces of Oppression" (State University of New York Press: 2014), Iris Marion Young wrote, "The advantaged, the dominant and the privileged, who hold positions of power in the United States, would not choose the term oppression to name injustice upon the oppressed in our society. Yet, injustice towards members of oppressed minority groups refers primarily to the use of diverse and ubiquitous forms of power in order to create, to maintain and to sustain diverse and ubiquitous forms of oppression, means the disabling of and the constraints for the oppressed, in tandem with the cultural, economic, educational, judicial, legal, legislative, political, religious, and social domination of oppressed minority groups across the United States." Renita Seabrook and Heather Wyatt-Nichol wrote in "The Ugly Side of America: Institutional Oppression and Race" (2016). "Historical accounts of American institutions and hence institutional; structures and hence structural; systems and hence systemic oppression in the United States dates to Colonial Virginia. We contend that institutional, organizational, structural, and systemic oppression in American society today, is the result of institutional, organizational, structural and systemic oppression throughout American history."

In "Groups and Oppression" Hypatia (2006), Elanor Taylor wrote, "Oppression" is a form of injustice that occurs when one oppressed social group is subordinated while another dominant group with power is privileged. And oppression is maintained by a variety of different mechanisms including ethical, moral, religious, and social norms, stereotypes, and institutional, organizational, structural, and systemic rules.... that illegitimately cause material (economic, educational, judicial, legislative, mental, physical, political, and/or social damage, death, harm, hurt, loss, pain, and suffering) as deprivation in American life." In

"Enduring Injustice" (Cambridge Univ. Press: 2012), Captain Ibrahim Traore, President of Burkina Faso understood Elanor Jeff Spinner-Halev who wrote, "the problem for the oppressed is not just the injustices of the past. The oppressed also suffer from injustices in the present."

For instance, John Rawls wrote in "A Theory of Justice" (Harvard Univ. Press: 1971), "......in a just society the liberties of equal citizenship for the oppressed are taken as settled; the rights secured by justice for the oppressed are not subject to political bargaining or to the calculus of social interests of the advantaged and privileged dominant group who wields power...." Similarly, Martin Luther King wrote in "Stride Toward Freedom" (Harper & Bros: 1958), "True peace is not merely the absence of tension; it is the presence of justice."

Moreover, Eric Heinze wrote in "The Concept of Injustice" (Routledge: 2013), "When it comes to the oppression of the oppressed my aim is....to underscore the systemic, as opposed to the individualistic, random or isolated character of oppression as injustice, as something rooted in the historical, economic, educational, judicial, legal, legislative, political, and social context." In "The Concept of Injustice" (Routledge: 2013), Eric Heinze wrote, "When it comes to the oppression of the oppressed, there is the concept of a dialectical relationship between justice and injustice which recognizes institutionalized, organized, structural, and systemic injustice pervading the social order in American society." In addition, Elanor Jeff Spinner-Halev wrote in "Enduring Injustice" (Cambridge Univ. Press: 2012), "the problem for the oppressed is not just the injustices of the past. The oppressed also suffer from injustices in the present in American society." Eric Heinze who wrote in "The Concept of Injustice" (Routledge: 2013), "when it comes to the oppression of the oppressed my aim is.... to underscore the systemic, as opposed to the individualistic, random or isolated character of oppression as injustice, as something rooted in the historical, economic, educational, judicial, legal, legislative, political, and social context."

In "The Concept of Injustice" (Routledge: 2013), Eric Heinze wrote, "When it comes to the oppression of the oppressed, there is the concept of a dialectical relationship between justice and injustice which recognizes institutionalized, organized, structural, and systemic injustice pervading the social order in American society."

David Miller wrote in " The Concept of Justice," in "The Stanford Encyclopedia of Philosophy" (Spring 2025), "For the oppressed, the concept of justice occupies center stage in ethics, morality, economic, legal, political, religious, political and social philosophy. The concept of justice is applied to patterns applied to both collective and individual actions, activities, behaviors and events, as well as to local, municipal, state and federal laws, ordinances, and statutes and to local, municipal, state and federal public policies. And we think, when it comes to oppressing the oppressed, in each case that if patterns of laws, ordinances, statutes and public policies are unjust this is a strong, maybe even a conclusive reason to reject them, when it comes to using patterns of power to oppress the oppressed in any society." Moreover, in "A Theory of Justice" (Harvard Univ. Press: 1971), John Rawls wrote, "When it comes to the oppressed, all social values—freedom, liberty, rights, opportunity, income and wealth, and the basis of self- respect—are to be distributed diversely, equally, equitably and hence fairly in American life." To be sure, Elanor Williams remarked, "The nation that insists on a society of law and order, without giving prior attention to justice, arbitrarily demands submission to tyranny."

But Iris Marion Young wrote in "Responsibility for Justice" (Oxford: 2014), "Structural injustice, then, exists when social processes put oppressed groups of persons under systematic threat of domination or deprivation of the means to develop and exercise their capacities, at the same time that these processes enable others to dominate or to have a wide range of opportunities for developing and exercising capacities available to the dominant group. Structural injustice is a kind of ethical and moral wrong against members of oppressed minority groups distinct from the wrongful actions, activities, behaviors and conduct of an individual agent or the repressive policies of a state. Structural injustice occurs as a consequence of many individuals and institutions acting to pursue their particular goals and interests, for the most part within the limits of accepted rules and norms."

Angus Stevenson wrote in "The Oxford Dictionary of English" (Oxford: 2010), "The concept, "stability," is defined as "the absence of disruption." For example, Erik W. Aslaksen wrote in "The Stability of Society" (Springer: 2020), "The concept, "society," is used to describe a wide range of associations between persons and/or persons of different, dissimilar and diverse groups we shall take the concept, "society," to be understood as "nation" or as "world." The International Encyclopedia of Social Sciences wrote in "Social Stability" The International Encyclopedia of Social Sciences (2015), "Social stability refers to a state of collective stability in a society, where agreements about norms are more likely to be developed and observed equally, equitably, fairy, impartially and justly." John Rawls wrote in "A Theory of Justice" (Harvard Univ. Press: 1971), "The stability of a society rests upon basic patterns of equality, equity, fairness, impartiality, justice, and social justice of its institutions, organizations, structures and systems towards the oppressed."

In "Existence is Resistance: Supporting Student-Led Social Change" Learning for Social Justice.org (20 March 2019), Stef Bernal-Martinez wrote. "There is always the tendency to place social action exclusively in the past. We teach about the Civil Rights Movement as a finality and not one of many histories of resistance in American society." Mona Lilja wrote in "The Definition of Resistance" Journal of Political Power (2022), "The sustained focus on either collective resistance (identity, framing, resource mobilization or strategy) or the forces of the 'everyday' and often hidden resistance is currently being negotiated by social science scholars, who are gradually identifying new forms of resistance on the spectrum between revolutionary uprisings and everyday forms of 'hidden' dissent." Mona Lilja wrote in "The Definition of Resistance" Journal of Political Power (2022), "It could be argued that in the contemporary situation, resistance is to be treated as an umbrella concept that contains forms of everyday, serial and organized resistance as well as the connection between these. In addition, the winding path of resistance studies and its interactions with different paradigms has led to that power and resistance are now 'widely seen as "entangled" rather than simply opposed'..."

Jason Brennan wrote in "When All Else Fails: The Ethics of Resistance to State Injustice" (Princeton Univ. Press: 2019), "Almost everyone today recognizes that law and justice are not the same thing; laws can be deeply unjust. Instead of exit, voice, or loyalty, this book defends the fourth option: resistance. My view is that forms, methods, strategies, tactics and techniques of resistance are justified in the face of power used to create, to maintain, and to sustain the oppression of the oppressed in American society." In addition, Bronwyne Davies wrote in the "Forward" in "The Politics of Recognition and Social Justice"

(Oxford: 2014), edited by Maria Pallota-Chiarolli and Bob Peace, "How do we think about resistance, social change and social justice?" In "The Definition of Resistance" Journal of Political Power (2022), Mona Lilja wrote, "More generally, we must discuss the relationality between power and resistance and how resistance emerges in relation to power. Or as expressed by H. Malmvig who wrote in "Eyes Wide Shut: Power and Creative Visual Counter-Conducts in the Battle for Syria" Global Society (2011–2014/2016), "'the chain metaphor might be expanded to include the power resistance relation, in so far as power and resistance circulate together and are mutually constitutive'."

Vassilios Zaikas wrote in "Rethinking Events" (Edward Algar: 2024), "A popular response," to interpreting "actions, activities, behaviors, and events as "unique," "is the notion of legacy, which has yet proven vague, not real, and misleading, serving primarily the interests of elites and the political-rhetoric expediency. The solution here is to shift focus from individuals who stand alone to large-scale multiple actions, activities, behaviors, and illustrative events by multiple home-grown actions, activities, behaviors, and events driven by bottom-up initiatives in a society."

Maurice Waite wrote in "Paperback Oxford English Dictionary"(Oxford: 2012), the concept, "unique," is defined as "actions, activities, behaviors, and events which are often unprecedented and therefore impossible to copy, to duplicate, to emulate, to imitate and to mimic." Angus Stevenson wrote in "The Oxford Dictionary of English" (Oxford: 2010), "The concept, "unparalleled," is defined as "actions, activities, behaviors, and events which are exceptional because they have no parallel or equal. Maurice Waite wrote in "Paperback Oxford Dictionary of English" (Oxford: 2012), "The concept "precedent," is defined as "earlier action, activity, behavior, propaganda, and events in the past taken as examples, models, and paradigms for situations in the future."

To be sure, Juan Williams wrote in "New Prize For These Eyes: The Rise of America's Second Civil Rights Movement" (Simon & Schuster: 2025), "Today's social movements are dealing with new realities, yet the truth is that civil rights activism is never quite finished." Further, it is reported "Around 2,000 communities nationwide plan to protest.... Data suggests protests in 2025 have increased compared to previous presidencies...." Yet, this work will clearly show that it will be difficult if not impossible to copy, to duplicate and/or to repeat the Civil Rights Movement. This is because the Cicil Rights Movement was unique, unparalleled, and without precedent.

CHAPTER 3

THE PROBLEM OF METHODS, STRATEGIES, TACTICS, TECHNIQUES OF PROTEST, RESISTANCE, CHARACTER, COURAGE & THE STATUS DUO

I t will be difficult if not impossible to copy, to duplicate and/or to repeat the Civil Rights Movement. This is because the leaders as well as student-leaders and children in the Civil Rights Movement came face-to-face with the contradiction and the problem of character, courage, the status quo and methods, strategies, tactics and techniques of protest and resistance.

Noam Chomsky remarked, "....real freedom....is neither a gift nor performance. It is a product of collective struggle, mutual responsibility, and the long often arduous work of democracy...Freedom is the struggle against the exercise of power against the public for the benefit of private interests. It is about the calculated mobilization of ignorance and fear and to restrict the freedom of the oppressed when lies become reality."

Angus Stevenson wrote in "The Oxford Dictionary of English" (Oxford: 2010), "The concept, "struggle," is defined as "the action, activity, behavior, conduct and events of fighting for something." Angus Stevenson wrote in "The Oxford Dictionary of English" (Oxford: 2010), "The concept, "courage," is defined as "the ability and the capacity to do and/or to endure dangerous, deadly, difficult and unpleasant actions, activities, behaviors, circumstances, contexts, events and situations." Angus Stevenson wrote in "The Oxford Dictionary of English" (Oxford: 2010), "The concept, "protest," is defined as "the action, activity, behavior, conduct and events of capturing and seizing a historical moment in order to make a strong objection and to make a strong demand while attending and taking part in loud, harsh and noisy boycotting, demonstrating, economic withdrawals, marching and sit-ins." In "The Oxford Dictionary of English" (Oxford: 2010), Angus Stevenson wrote, "The concept, "resistance," is defined as "the action, activity, behavior, conduct and events of refusal to abide by, to accommodate, to act in accordance with, to adhere to, to agree with, to comply, to conform, to follow, to obey, to observe, and/or to respect." Angus Stevenson and Maurice Waite wrote in "Concise Oxford Dictionary" (Oxford: 2011), "The concept, "change," is defined variously as "actions, activities, behaviors and events which causes a society to undergo reconstruction."

Howard Thurman remarked, "You must lay your lives on the altar of social change so that wherever you are there the Kingdom of God is at hand!" Leaders as well as student- leaders and children in the Civil Rights Movement understood Howard Thurman who wrote in "Jesus and the Disinherited" (Beacon Press: 1949), "Uniqueness always escapes us when we undertake to do an analysis of character." For instance, Thomas A. Wright wrote in "What is Character and Why It Really Does Matter" Fordham University.edu (Winter 2013), "A person and/or group of persons who exhibits moral discipline if they suppress personal needs for those of a greater societal good. The second dimension of character is moral attachment. Moral attachment constitutes a clear affirmation of a person and/or group of persons commitment to someone or to something greater than themselves. The third dimension is moral autonomy. A person and/or group of people exhibits moral autonomy if they have the capacity to freely make ethical, character-based decisions. Autonomy means that a person and/or group of people have both the necessary discretion and the skills of judgment at their disposal to freely act morally. Building on these three dimensions, character can be defined as internal and habitual qualities within a person and/or group of people and individuals, and applicable to organizations that both constrain and lead them to desire and pursue personal and societal good." Further, Theresa Boyd who wrote in "The Meaning of Courage" Penn State

University.edu (09 June 2016), "When we hear of a person and/or a group of persons being called a "hero"—as is common these days—that person and/or a group of persons have committed acts of courage."

Moreover, Cynthia L. S. Pury and Amber A. Mulkey who wrote in "Courage" Encyclopedia of Personality and Individual Differences" (2020), "In addition to the two competing definitions of courage, this entry reviews different common subtypes of courage – physical, moral, and vital/psychological courage – as well as a distinction between courage as an accolade and courage as a process. Two different definitions of courage are common in the psychological literature: courage as an approach despite fear and courage as noble action taken voluntarily and despite risk."

To be sure, leaders, as well as student-leaders and children in the\ Civil Rights Movement understood Howard Thurman who wrote in "Temptations of Jesus" (Lawton Kennedy: 1962), "Institutions, organizations, structures and systems of oppression always fight back. This is because institutions, organizations, structures and systems of oppression do not want to be upset because they prefer the status quo in American life." For example, Emma A. Bäck and Torun Lindholm wrote in "Defending or Challenging the Status Quo" Journal of Social and Political Psychology (2014), "Institutions, organizations, structures, systems and societies are in constant transition, evolving and changing from one form to another. At the same time, when it comes to oppression and to the oppressed, the dominant group with access to the exercise of diverse forms of power usually prefer keeping things the way they are, and resist institutional, organizational, structural and systemic change in American society." In "Defending or Challenging the Status Quo" Journal of Social and Political Psychology (2014), Emma A. Bäck and Torun Lindholm wrote, "As the default ideological position is conservative and is conservative status quo maintaining, proponents of institutional, organizational, structural and systemic change are often met with violent backlash and opposition. According to system justification theory, the conservative motivation to prefer the status quo is the conservative motivation to enhance oneself and one's dominant group who possess access to the exercise of diverse forms of power. This implies that it may take more of an effort and a risk to challenge the status quo than to support its existence."

In terms of the status quo during the Civil Rights Movement, William Faulkner wrote in "Letter to a Northern Editor" (05 March 1956), "I would say to leaders, as well as student-leaders and children in the Civil Rights Movement, and all the organizations who would compel immediate and unconditional integration: Go slow now. Stop—just for a moment. Pause there, just for a while."

To leaders as well as student-leaders and children in the Civil Rights Movement, Howard Thurman wrote in "Deep River: The Negro Spiritual Speaks of Life and Death" (Friends United Press: 1945/1978), "These essays are sent on their way in order to provide the readers with an assist in their struggle for courage, for self-respect and for emotional stability." To be sure on the one hand, to leaders as well as student-leaders and children in the Civil Rights Movement, Robert F, Williams wrote in "Negroes with Guns" (Marzani & Munsell: 1962), "The Afro-American militant is a 'militant' because he defends himself, his family, his home, and his dignity. He does not introduce violence into a racist social system - the violence is already there and has always been there. It is precisely this unchallenged violence that allows a racist social system to perpetuate itself. When people say that they are opposed to Negroes 'resorting to violence' what they really mean is that they are opposed to Negroes defending themselves and challenging the exclusive monopoly of violence practiced by white racists." To leaders as well as student-leaders and children in the Civil Rights Movement, Howard Thurman wrote in "Jesus and the Disinherited" (1949), "For those who protest and who resist, violence is often the last resort. This is because, in oppressed communities, the cries of desperation can be heard: "We must do something!" "Something must be done!"" Martin Luther King remarked, "Every human being of humane convictions must decide on the protest and the resistance that best suits his convictions, but we must all protest and resist."

For example, leaders as well as student-leaders and children in the Civil Rights Movement, understood Howard Thurman who wrote in "Jesus and the Disinherited" (Beacon Press: 1949), "For the purpose of our discussion, resistance is defined as an overt expression of an inner attitude. Again and again, it has been demonstrated that the lines are held by those whose hold on security is sure as long as the status quo remains intact. Moreover, there will always be opposition to effective protest because effective protests upset the status quo." Leaders as well as student-leaders and children in the Civil Rights Movement, understood Howard Thurman who wrote in "Jesus and the Disinherited" (Beacon Press: 1949), "There will be attendant loss of life, loss of limb, loss of livelihood, loss of reputation, loss of mental wellbeing and loss of physical wellbeing. For those who accept this, there may be quick and speedy judgement. But if the number increases and the movement for justice and social justice for the oppressed spreads, the vindication of reality will follow in its wake in American society."

Leaders as well as student-leaders and children in the Civil Rights Movement, understood Howard Thurman who wrote in ""The Search for Common Ground" (1971.1986), "There are those who think that protest and resistance will be terminated by 'Law and Order without Justice.'"" It is reported Captain Ibrahim Traore, President of Burkina Faso remarked, "They keep telling me I will die like Gaddafi, Thomas Sankara, or any young leader that tried to make Africa better. I am not scared, and I will never regret dying for my people. If I must die for this freedom, I will die standing tall."

CHAPTER 4

THE PROBLEM OF OUTSIDERS, COMMUNITY AND MASS ORGANIZING

It will be difficult, if not impossible, to copy, duplicate and/or repeat in the Civil Rights Movement. This is because leaders as well as student-leaders and children in the Civil Rights Movement came face- to-face with the contradiction and the problem of being outsiders, creating community, organizing, maintaining and sustaining the oppressed masses."

For example, Graham Scambler wrote in "A Sociology of Shame and Blame: Insider versus Outsider" (Palgrave Macmillan: 2020), "It is not possible to identify the oppressed who are outsiders as normal, able-bodied, ethical, moral, responsible, healthy, law-abiding, or as insiders who belong and as a host of other positives, unless it is also possible for the oppressed in the same society. Yet, it is possible to identify the oppressed as abnormal, amoral, criminal, defective, deviant disabled, immoral, irresponsible, the worst of the worst and unethical outsiders or as strangers." For example, on the one hand, it is reported that Captain Ibrahim Traore remarked. "To my brothers and sisters in America, I see your pain, I see your struggle...the land you helped build, with blood and sweat, now, chokes you with laws and bullets. You are told you are free, yet you are watched. You are told that you are equal, yet you are feared. You are told that you belong. Yet you are treated as outsiders."

Nevertheless, leaders as well as student-leaders and children in the Civil Rights Movement were able to create community because they understood Howard Thurman who wrote in "The Search for Common Ground" (Friends United Press: 1971/1986), "For Negroes, all doors outside their communities were closed to them." Yet, Howard Thurman who wrote in "The Search for Common Ground" (Friends United Press: 1971/1986), "Every human being has an organic need to care for and to be cared for...to love and to be loved...to understand and\to be understood...which is the essential stuff of community beyond the white dualism of whether or not Black lives are good or evil." Moreover, Howard Thurman wrote in "The Search for Common Ground" (Harper & Bros: 1971), leaders as well as student-leaders and children in the Civil Rights Movement ".... were members of organic communities which provided them with a sense of belonging and provided then with a cause more important than whether they lived died. No amount of argumentation, logic, and rationalization could turn them around."

Again, it is reported that Captain Ibrahim Traore remarked. "If I must die for this freedom, I will die standing tall." Similarly, Diane Nash relentlessly remarked, "We know that we may be killed. Therefore, we signed our last will and testament last night." In the same way, Martin Luther King relentlessly remarked, "I'd rather be a coward than a corpse and dead rather than afraid. I am not scared of death; I am willing to pay the ultimate price for my people." In the same way, Fannie Lou Hamer relentlessly remarked, "In this America, the land of the free and the home of the brave, the oppressed must sleep with our telephones off of the hooks because our lives be threatened daily, But, when they asked for the oppressed to raise their hands and asked "Who'd go down to the courthouse the next day, where the burn the oppressed alive as they are hanging from a tree on the courthouse lawn?" I raised mine. Had it as high up as I could get it. I guess if I'd had any sense, I would have been a little scared, but what was the point of being scared? The only thing the oppressors could do to me was kill me and it seemed like they'd been trying to do that a little bit at a time ever since I could remember."

In addition, Malcolm X relentlessly remarked, "We're not outnumbered. We're out organized. Yet only those who have already experienced a revolution within themselves can reach out effectively to help others. You're living at a time of extremism, a time of revolution, A time where there's got to be a change. People in power have misused it. And now there has to be a change and a better world has to be built. And the only way it is going to be built is with extreme methods And I for one will join with anyone, don't care what color you are. If you want to change this miserable condition that exists on this earth" Moreover, in the same way Fred Hampton relentlessly remarked, "You can jail revolutionaries, but you can't jail the revolution." In the same way Huey P. Newton relentlessly remarked, "Laws should be made to serve the people. People should not be made to serve the law. Thus, my fear was not of death itself, but a death without meaning. The first lesson a revolutionary must learn is that he is a doomed man in American society." And, in the same way, Stokely Carmichel (Kwame Toure) relentlessly remarked, "Our grandfathers had to run, run, run. My generation's out of breath. We aren't running anymore. And mass movements that produce non-random institutional, organic, structural and systematic social change are always organized from the bottom up."

CHAPTER 5

THE PROBLEM OF HUMAN RIGHTS
AND SELF-DETERMINATION

It will be difficult, if not impossible to copy, to duplicate and/or repeat the Civil Rights Movement. This is because leaders as well as student-leaders and children in the Civil Rights Movement came face-to-face with the contradiction and the problem of human rights and self-determination.

For example, Omar Dahbour wrote in "Self-Determination in Political Philosophy and International Law" History of European Ideas (1993), "Self-determination as a political concept dates from the early years of this century, but its origins lie in eighteenth- and nineteenth-century philosophy. The idea of self- determination originated as a notion of the freedom of individuals to determine the conditions of their own life. It's later expansion to include the self-determination of communities as well as individuals has been characterized as a shift of concern from 'personhood' to 'peoplehood'." Hurst Hannum wrote in "The Right of Self-Determination in the Twenty-First Century "Washington & Lee Law Review (01 June 1998) "For members of oppressed minority groups, self-determination "is" a human right. Although there are many hortatory references to self-determination in "General Assembly" resolutions and elsewhere, the only legally binding documents in which the right of self-determination for the oppressed is proclaimed are the two international covenants.' The first paragraph of common article 1 states: "All oppressed people have the right of self-determination. By virtue of that right they freely determine their political status and freely pursue their economic, social and cultural development." See "International Covenant on Civil and Political Rights" Dec. 19, 1966, art. 1, 999 U.N.T.S. 171; "International Covenant on Economic, Social and Cultural Rights" Dec. 16, 1966, art.1, 993 U.N.T.S. 3.

Moreover, Michael Freeman wrote in "The Right to Self-Determination: Philosophical and Legal Perspectives" New England Journal of Public Policy (20 Nov 2019), "The most familiar, and the primary legal, definition of self-determination is that of the common article 1 of the 1966 International Covenant on Economic, Social and Cultural Rights and the International Covenant on Civil and Political Rights. It reads as follows: All oppressed minority groups have the right to self-determination. By virtue of that right, they freely determine their political status and freely pursue their economic, social and cultural development." Quoted in Ian Brownlie, Editor, "Basic Documents on Human Rights," 3rd Edition (Clarendon Press: 1992). In addition, Michael Freeman wrote in "The Right to Self-Determination: Philosophical and Legal Perspectives" New England Journal of Public Policy (20 Nov 2019), "Orthodox human rights theory maintains that the complete fulfilment of human rights for the oppressed, would be sufficient to protect the rights of members of these oppressed minority groups. Others argue that experience shows that, in the absence of collective guaranteed and protected freedoms, liberties and rights, the individual rights of members of vulnerable oppressed minority groups will in practice be insecure, in American life."

James Nickel and Adam Etinson wrote in "Human Rights" in "The Stanford Encyclopedia of Philosophy "(Fall 2024), "Human rights are norms that aspire to protect all people everywhere from severe political, legal, and social abuses, harms and injuries. Examples of human rights are the right to freedom of religion, the right to a fair trial when charged with a crime, the right not to be tortured, and the right to education. The philosophy of human rights addresses questions about the existence, content, nature, universality, justification, and legal status of human rights. The strong claims often made on behalf of human rights (for example, that they are universal, inalienable, or exist independently of legal enactment as justified moral norms)." In addition, in "Human Rights" in "The Stanford Encyclopedia of Philosophy "(Fall 2024), James Nickel and Adam Etinson wrote, "Lest we miss the obvious, human rights are rights focus on freedom, protection, status, immunity, or benefit for the rights holder. Most human rights are claim rights that impose duties or responsibilities on duty bearers. The duties associated with human rights often require actions involving respect, protection, facilitation, and provision in any society."

Moreover, The United Nations Human Rights Report wrote in "The Right to Adequate Food: Fact Sheet No. 34" OHCHR.org (April 2010), "Human rights are interdependent, indivisible and interrelated. This means that violating the right to food may impair the enjoyment of other human rights, such as the right to health, education or life, and vice versa...."

CHAPTER 6

THE PROBLEM OF RIGHTS, SUCCESS, FAILURE AND BACKLASH

It will be difficult, if not impossible to copy, to duplicate and/or repeat the Civil Rights Movement. This is because leaders as well as student-leaders and children in the Civil Rights Movement came face-to-face with the contradiction and the problem of rights, success, failure and backlash.

Leaders as well as student-leaders and children in the Civil Rights Movement understood Howard Thurman who wrote in "Meditations of the Heart" (Friends United Press: 1953), "In a sense, all of living is a struggle between the will to live and the will to die. Again, there are some things in life that are worse than death." For instance, Diane Nash remarked, "We wanted social movements for justice and for social justice which would outlast our lives. Sir, you should know, we all signed our last wills and testaments last night before they left [on the bus for Birmingham, Alabama]. We know someone will be killed. But we cannot let violence overcome nonviolence.""

For instance, in "Police and Protests" LDF Thurgood Marshall Insitute.org (2021), Sandhya Kajeepeta and Daniel K.N. Johnson wrote, "For the oppressed, in addition to being essential for democracy, the right to protest has been essential for Black lives' struggle for racial justice in the U.S. Countless historic civil rights victories have been achieved in part through the attention and pressure created through sustained, organized public protests demanding progress on pressing issues of the times. Notable protests during the Civil Rights Movement include the Montgomery Bus Boycott of 1955-56 and the Selma to Montgomery March in 1965, among many other examples. The Montgomery Bus Boycott played a key role in Browder v. Gayle, where the Supreme Court ruled that racial segregation on public buses was unconstitutional. The Selma March was part of a broader campaign for equal voting access and contributed to the passage of the Voting Rights Act of 1965. These historic events exemplify how the right to protest played an instrumental role in the Civil Rights Movement."

Of course, because of the pervasiveness of violence, leaders as well as student-leaders and children in the Civil Rights Movement understood that protest and resistance was, in the final analysis, a kind of suicide, as it were. For instance, leaders as well as student-leaders and children in the Civil Rights Movement understood James R. McGovern who wrote in "Anatomy of a Lynching: The Killing of Claude Neal" (Louisiana State University Press: 1982/2013), "While the murders of oppressed Black lives were personal deeds, spectacle lynching in the sense of a public execution of another person by a self-constituted group with accompanying public rituals, is a collective and social act terrorism. Further, spectacle lynchings as public execution as white supremacist domestic terrorism requires confidence in white community approval in American society."

Michael Cholbi wrote in "Suicide" in "The Stanford Encyclopedia of Philosophy" (Winter 2024), "what is it to intend that death result from one's behavior? Throughout history, suicide has evoked an astonishingly wide range of reactions—bafflement, dismissal, heroic glorification, sympathy, anger, moral or religious condemnation, but it is never uncontroversial. For example, suicide has long been a central concern within many academic disciplines, including sociology, anthropology, psychology, and psychiatry." In addition, Michael Cholbi wrote in "Suicide" in "The Stanford Encyclopedia of Philosophy" (Winter 2024), "perhaps the most enduring controversies surrounding suicide are philosophical. For philosophers, suicide raises a host of conceptual, moral, and psychological questions. Among these questions are: What makes a person's behavior suicidal? What motivates such behavior? Is suicide morally permissible, or even morally required in some extraordinary circumstances? Is suicidal behavior rational? Is aiding others to commit suicide morally permissible or even required in some extraordinary circumstances?"

There are those who argue that leaders as well as student-leaders and children in the Civil Rights Movement "failed." Yet, Martin Luther King remarked, "It may be true that federal laws cannot and will not change hearts. But federal laws can restrain the heartless. Federal laws can restrain being beaten and killed by police officers. And federal laws can prevent me from being lynched."

We may say with accuracy and with precision that leaders, as well student-leaders and children in the Civil Rights Movement secured "the action potential" of the following U.S. Constitutional freedoms, liberties and rights for members of oppressed minority groups in American life. For example, a recent "AI Overview: The Concept of Governance" (2025) wrote, "The concept, "governance," in its simplest form, refers to the processes and systems by which decisions are made and implemented. It encompasses the mechanisms through which power is exercised, resources are managed, and societal needs are addressed. Beyond government, governance involves a range of actors, including state institutions, civil society, and the private sector, working together to achieve common goals."

Malcolm X wrote in "The Autobiography of Malcolm X" (Grove Press: 1965), "And when I speak, I don't speak as a Democrat or a Republican, nor an American. I speak as a victim of America's so-called democracy. You and I have never seen democracy – all we've seen re contradictions." Martin Luther King remarked "Even when the polls are open to all, Negroes have shown themselves too slow to exercise their voting privileges. There must be a concerted effort on the part of Negro leaders to arouse their people from their apathetic indifference."

Howard Thurman wrote in "Luminous Darkness: A Personal Interpretation of the Anatomy of Segregation" (Harper: 1965), "Based on our U.S. Constitutional form government, it is not the prerogative of any group to decide who is and who is not a citizen....Once an American feels that America is not his ho0meland, he has given up his right to claim the fruits of citizenship. This right must be maintained at all costs because it is lost in the spirit of Negroes, then the door to citizenship closes in his own heart and all is lost. It would mean that the external denial of citizenship as expressed in segregation becomes internalized and all is lost." Yet, the effective protests and resistance which was implemented by leaders as well as student-leaders and children in the Civil Rights Movement provided members of oppressed minority groups with the potential of experiencing United States Constitutionally guaranteed freedoms, liberties and rights of "citizenship."

For example, on the one hand, in 1857, in the "Dred Scott" case, the United States Supreme Court decided that "....because Black men are inferior and white men are superior, the Black man has no freedoms, liberties or rights which the white man is bound to respect." Yet, on the other hand, Dominique Leydet wrote in "Citizenship" in The Stanford Encyclopedia of Philosophy (Fall 2023), "A citizen is a member of a political community who enjoys the guaranteed and protected freedoms, liberties and rights of that political community in a democracy." In addition, in "What Is Citizenship, and What Fruits Can It Bear?" PA Times.org (21 March 2021), Christopher Frank Rondinelli wrote, "....the cornerstone of citizenship, is defined by Tina Nabatchi as, "The activities by which people's concerns, needs, interests and values are incorporated into decisions and actions on public matters and issues."

Moreover, Rebecca Hamlin wrote in "Civil Rights" Encyclopedia Britannica (25 June 2025), "Civil rights are guaranteed and protected freedoms, liberties and rights with equal protection under law, regardless of disabilities, gender, nation of origin, race or religion Examples of civil rights include due process under law, the right to vote, the right to a fair trial, the right to government services, the right to a public education, and the right to use public facilities. Civil rights are an essential component of democracy; when the oppressed are being denied guaranteed and protected freedoms, liberties and rights with equal protection under law in political society, they are being denied their civil rights." Rebecca Hamlin wrote in "Civil Rights" Encyclopedia Britannica (25 June 2025),"....civil rights are secured by positive government action, often in the form of legislation. Civil rights laws attempt to guarantee full and equal citizenship for people who have traditionally been discriminated against on the basis of some group characteristic. When the enforcement of civil rights is found by many to be inadequate, a civil rights movement may emerge in order to call for equal application of the laws without discrimination."

The effective protests and resistance which was implemented by leaders as well as student-leaders and children in the Civil Rights Movement provided members of oppressed minority groups with the potential of experiencing "democracy." Robyn Hardyman wrote in "What Is A Democracy?" (Oxford: 2014), "In his Gettysburg Address, U.S. President Abraham Lincoln (1809- The effective protests and resistance which was implemented by leaders as well as student-leaders and children in the Civil Rights Movement provided members of oppressed minority groups with the potential of experiencing United States Constitutionally guaranteed freedoms, liberties and rights under "the rule of law." For example, Robert Stein wrote in "What Exactly is the Rule of Law?" Houston School of Law (2019), Robert Stein wrote, "The World Justice Project" whose definition of the rule of law is based on four universal principles: 1. Accountability: The government as well as private actors are accountable under the law. 2. Just Laws: The laws are clear, publicized, stable, and just; are applied evenly; and protect fundamental rights, including the security of persons, contract and property rights, and certain core human rights; Open Government: The processes by which the laws are enacted, administered, and enforced are accessible, fair, and efficient. 4. Accessible & Impartial Dispute Resolution: Justice is delivered timely by competent, ethical, and independent representatives and neutrals who are accessible, have adequate resources, and reflect the makeup of the communities they serve."

In "What Exactly is the Rule of Law?" Houston School of Law (2019), Robert Stein wrote, "The International Bar Association (IBA) has instead adopted "an authoritative statement on behalf of the world-wide egal profession [that] . . . sets out some of the essential characteristics of the Rule of Law . . . .These characteristics include: independent, impartial judiciary; the presumption of innocence; the right to a fair and public trial without undue delay; a rational and proportionate approach to punishment; a strong and independent legal profession; strict protection of confidential communications between lawyer and client; equality of all before the law . . . ." Jeremy Waldron wrote in "The Rule of Law.:

in "The Stanford Encyclopedia of Philosophy" (Winter 2023), "Rule of Law is one of the ideals of our political morality and it refers to the ascendancy of law as such and of the institutions of the legal system in a system of governance," and "The Rule of Law comprises a number of principles of a formal and procedural character, addressing the way in which a community is governed."

Of course, for members of oppressed minority groups, there is the problem of martial law. Howard Thurman wrote in "Jesus and the Disinherited" (Beacon Press: 1949), "When it comes to immigrants, there is the profound fear of and resistance against invasion of the church, the home and the school." For example, it is reported, "Martial law involves the temporary substitution of military authority for civilian rule and is usually invoked in time of war invasion, rebellion, revolt, unrest or natural disaster. When martial law is in effect, the military commander of an area or country has unlimited authority to make and enforce laws...." In "Martial Law in Times of Civil Disorder" Law and Order (Sept 1989), E. W. Killam wrote, "Martial law involves the temporary substitution of military authority for civilian rule and is usually invoked in time of war, rebellion, or natural disaster. When martial law is in effect, the military commander of an area or country has unlimited authority to make and enforce laws. Furthermore, martial law suspends all existing laws, as well as civil authority and the ordinary administration of justice. In the United States, martial law may be declared by proclamation of the President or a State governor, but such a formal proclamation is not necessary."

Further, Samuel Strom, J.D. wrote in "Martial Law in Times of Civil Disorder" Find Law (17 Aug 2024), "As noted above, the Constitution does not define martial law. Instead, its use throughout history has defined its application and limits. Generally speaking, it refers to when the military temporarily substitutes its authority in place of civilian authority. More simply, it occurs when the army takes over a civilian area and imposes its own rules." Samuel Strom, J.D. wrote in "Martial Law in Times of Civil Disorder" Find Law (17 Aug 2024), "According to national security law scholar Joseph Nunn, martial law "is a "dramatic departure from normal practice in the United States." Federal laws usually prevent the military from acting within the country. Although the president can call the military into action to help local governments after a natural disaster, like a hurricane, its help is usually limited. Martial law, as Nunn writes, "turns that relationship on its head," due to the government assuming governance of the area."

In "Police State, U.S.A." "The Independent Review (Fall 2021), Christopher J. Coyne and Yuliya Yatsyshins wrote, "Police states are typically defined by certain general characteristics—a highly centralized form of authoritarian government with few, if any, constraints, the prevalence of the state in all areas of socioeconomic life, corrupt elections, a state surveillance apparatus, misinformation operations, arbitrary detention without trial, a militarized domestic police force employed for social control, efforts to silence or censor dissent and the media, and a lack of respect for civil liberties and human rights." In "The Problem of State Violence" American Academy of Arts & Sciences (2022), Paul Butler wrote, "It is easy to see state violence in the U.S. Department of Defense "1033 Program," which provides "surplus" military equipment like armored tanks, grenade launchers, and bayonets for local police departments to use against members of oppressed minority groups. Likewise, many recognize state violence in the facts that police use of force is the sixth leading cause of death of men between the ages of twenty-five and twenty-nine, and that one in one thousand oppressed Black men are killed by the state sanctioned violence of police in American society."

In "The Rise of the "Illegal Alien"" Contexts (2013), Edwin. Ackerman wrote, "The language of illegality has permeated the conversation about immigration in the past decades to the extent that arguments have become tautological: illegal aliens should not be legalized because they are illegal. In the country's last full-blown debate on the issue—the Senate's contemplation of an "amnesty bill" in 2006—both sides of the aisle argued whether granting legal status to undocumented immigrants constituted a "reward" for lawbreakers...." In "The Rise of the "Illegal Alien"" Contexts (2013), Edwin R. Ackerman wrote, "The prevalence of the adjective "illegal" to describe unauthorized immigration is a fixture of the last quarter of the 20th century. According to legal scholar Gerald Newman, prior to 1950, there is no mention of the word "illegal" in judicial decisions concerning immigration. A look at Gallup poll questions going back to 1936 shows that "illegal" immigration was not part of any questionnaire until 1977. And, as a social geographer. Joseph Nevins has documented, in 1924, when the Border Patrol was born, the most commonly used term in major newspapers was simply "aliens." By 1954, during the time of Operation Wetback, "illegal" was used in only a quarter of references to unauthorized immigration. In 1977 the term "illegal alien" was present in 76% of the references. It was in 1994, during the controversy over Proposition 187 in California, that the term reached saturation. With the law, which called for suspension of public services to persons lacking documentation, we saw the term "illegal" in 90% of the cases."

Moreover, Hidetaka Hirota wrote in "Expelling the Poor: The Antebellum Origins of American Deportation Policy" Gilder Lehrman. org (Fall 2028), "Dehumanizing insults to foreigners, aggressive enforcement of immigration law by overzealous officials, and tragic family separation routinely appear in immigration-related news in the United States today. At the center of the present immigration debate is deportation policy. While current deportation policy primarily targets undocumented immigrants, the legal system of expelling foreigners itself is deeply rooted in American history, perhaps more deeply than most Americans would think." Sondra Crosby wrote in "Forced Displacement of Migrants Is Cruel and Inhumane—the United States Must Do Better" BU.edu (01 Feb 2023), "As a physician, I see the impact of forced displacement every day in my refugee practice. I have listened to countless narratives of unspeakable suffering. When we view people as "less than human," it is easier to look the other way and to legitimize horrific behavior such as the Native American genocide, slavery, and the barbarity of World War II." Further, Hidetaka Hirota wrote in "Expelling the Poor: The Antebellum Origins of American Deportation Policy" Gilder Lehrman.org (Fall\ 2028), "It is now relatively well known that the Chinese Exclusion Act of 1882, which banned the admission of Chinese laborers, was the first federal legislation that had a deportation provision. The law made deportable Chinese laborers who entered the nation in violation of the act. Yet this hardly means that no deportation law existed in the United States prior to federal Chinese exclusion. The origins of American immigration restriction lay in antebellum state-level policies on the Atlantic seaboard, which were driven partly by cultural prejudice against destitute Irish immigrants but even more fundamentally by economic concerns about their poverty and dependency."

The effective protests and resistance which was implemented by leaders as well as student-leaders and children in the Civil Rights

Movement provided members of oppressed minority groups with the potential of experiencing United States Constitutionally guaranteed freedoms, liberties and rights such as "habeas corpus." For instance, John H. Blume and David P. Voisin wrote in "An Introduction to Federal Habeas Corpus Practice and Procedure" Cornell University Law Review (Winter 1996), "For many prisoners, federal habeas corpus stands as the last opportunity to challenge the constitutionality of their convictions or sentences. Simply navigating through the procedural maze of habeas practice, however, is a formidable task for inmates proceeding pro se and prisoners represented by counsel. Tragically, those who have had a fundamentally unfair trial, and even those who are innocent, may easily stumble. Since the Reconstruction year of 1867, habeas corpus, or the Great Writ, has been available to state prisoners "in all cases where any person may be restrained of his or her liberty in violation of the constitution, or of any treaty or law of the United States." The modern era of federal habeas corpus, however, did not begin until the Supreme Court's decision in Brown v. Allen. In Brown, the Court held that the violation of a constitutional right is cognizable in federal habeas and that federal courts may independently review state court adjudications of federal questions, even if the state court's treatment of those legal claims was full and fair."

The effective protests and resistance which was implemented by leaders as well as student-leaders and children in the Civil Rights Movement provided members of oppressed minority groups with the potential of experiencing United States Constitutionally guaranteed freedoms, liberties and rights such as "due process of law." For example, W. J. Brockelbank wrote in Role of Due Process in American Constitutional Law" Cornell Law Quarterly (Summer 1954), "The U.S. Constitution provides that compensation for the taking of private property must be just, that the protection of the laws must be equal, that punishments must be neither cruel nor unusual, that fines must not be excessive, that searches and seizures must not be unreasonable and that one must not be deprived of life, liberty or property without due process of law." W. J. Brockelbank wrote in Role of Due Process in American Constitutional Law" Cornell Law Quarterly (Summer 1954), "After the U.S. Supreme Court of the United States held in 1833 that the Fifth Amendment was binding only on the federal government, we find "due process" turning up in the Reconstruction Fourteenth Amendment adopted after the

Civil War and expressly made applicable to the states by the following words: "Nor shall any state deprive any person of life, liberty or property without due process of\ law."

The effective protests and resistance which was implemented by leaders as well as student-leaders and children in the Civil Rights Movement provided members of oppressed minority groups with the potential of experiencing United States Constitutionally guaranteed freedoms, liberties and rights such as "law and order." In "Law and Order" Annual Review of Law and Social Science (2022), Nick Cheeseman wrote, "This American yearning for law and order as the reassertion of safety and security in the face of perceived social decay and upheaval dates at least to early-modern formulations of law and order as David Garland wrote in "The Culture of Control: Crime and Social Order in Contemporary Society" (Univ. Chicago Press: 2001), "....the suppression of alternative powers and competing sources of justice as well as the control of crime and disorderly conduct" through the exercise of sovereign power over the lives of the oppressed in American society." A recent "AI Overview: The Concept of Law and Order" (2025) wrote, "The "law and order" concept, often used in political discourse, refers to the preservation of social order through the enforcement of laws, typically, with a focus on harsher penalties for crime. Academic research explores how this concept influences public opinion, shapes policy, and interacts with other legal ideals like the rule of law. Some scholars also examine the historical roots of law and order, including its relationship to concepts like colonial legal systems and the enforcement of injustices upon the oppressed...."

Elie Wiesel remarked "There may be times when the oppressed are powerless to prevent injustice, but there must never be a time when the oppressed to not make every effort to correct such injustice." W. E. B. Du Bois wrote in "The Souls of Black Folk" (Oxford: 1903/2010), "The problem of the twentieth century will be the problem of the color line." To be sure, there was the failure of "The First Reconstruction of Liberal American Democracy," after the end of the Civil War in 1865 and the end of Reconstruction in 1877. This failure prompted W.E.B. Du Bois to write in "Black Reconstruction in America, 1860-1880" (Free Press: 1935.1999), "The slave went free, stood a brief moment in the sun, then moved back again toward slavery."

In the aftermath of the Civil Rights Movement, Thurgood Marshall remarked. "Today's Constitution is a realistic document of freedom for the oppressed only because of several corrective amendments to the U.S. Constitution. Those amendments speak to a sense of decency and fairness that I and other Blacks cherish..." Nevertheless, we may say with accuracy and with precision that "backlash" consciously aimed to dismantle the success of protest and resistance implemented by leaders as well as student-leaders and children in the Civil Rights Movement.

To be sure, leaders, as well as student-leaders and children in the Civil Rights Movement pressured the U.S. House of Representatives, the U.S. Seante and the U.S. President to pass the federal Civil Rights Act in 1964; to pass the federal Voting Rights Act of 1965; and to pass the federal Fair Housing Act of 1968 Amendments to the U.S. Constitution. These federal laws allowed members of oppressed minority groups to "potentially" experience a liberal democracy, and constitutionally guaranteed and protected freedoms, liberties, and rights such as due process, the rule of law, law and order, legal representation according to law; the presumption of innocence; trial by a jury of one's peers; the absence of illegal searches and seizures; as well as the absence of cruel and unusual punishment; and equal protection of the law based on the equal protection clause of the Reconstruction Fourteenth Amendment to the U.S. Constitution proposed, passed and signed into formal law on June 13, 1866, and ratified by the U.S. Congress on July 9,1868.

Maurice Waite wrote in Paperback Oxford English Dictionary" (Oxford: 2012), "The concept, "backlash," is defined as "the action, activity, behavior, conduct and events of intense and strong, anger, bitterness, grievance, hatred, and resentment-filled and often violent reactions to change, especially towards oppressed minority groups by a large number of persons in a society." We may say with accuracy and with precision, that backlash consciously aimed to dismantle the Civil Rights Act in 1964, the Voting Rights Act of 1965; and the Fair Housing Act of 1968. For instance, Martin Luther King remarked, "Backlash a new name for an old phenomenon, in the history of American society."

In "Toward a Theory of Backlash: Dynamic Resistance and the Central Role of Power" Cambridge University.org (25 Nov 2008), Jane Mansbridge and Shauna L. Shames wrote, "In colloquial usage, "backlash" denotes politically conservative angry and bitter reactions to progressive (or liberal) economic, educational, legal, legislative, political and change for members of oppressed minority groups in American society." Further, in "Toward a Theory of Backlash: Dynamic Resistance and the Central Role of Power" Cambridge University.org (25 Nov 2008), Jane Mansbridge and Shauna L. Shames wrote, "Backlash" includes acts of genuine persuasion as well as acts of coercive, controlling and socially controlling power. We draw on the sociological literature on social movements and counter-movements as well as the political science literature on power, preferences, and interests. We focus mostly on examples drawn from the United States....We begin where the process of backlash itself begins, with the exercise of power because of a challenge to the status quo in American society."

In "The Racist Backlash Obama Faced During His Presidency" The Washington Post (22 April 2016), Terence Samuel wrote, "from the very beginning, Obama's ascendance produced a huge white backlash that was undeniably racist in nature...." In "The Enduring Backlash against Racial Justice in the United States" "Journal of Community Practice" (2021), Kelly Patterson et al wrote, 'We argue that opposition to federal civil rights legislation emerged as an organizing principle of the political right in the United States during the early 1960s. Although overlooked, this shift in political strategy is arguably one of the more successful policy agendas implemented during the contemporary period. Political conservatives, who constitute the right-wing in the United States, framed civil rights policies as failures from their inception, starved them of necessary fiscal resources, lobbied to reverse them, and defined social justice movements as undemocratic, unfair, and a subterfuge for patronage politics and clientelism." See Eric Chyn wrote in "Inequality and Racial Backlash: Evidence from the Freedmen's Bureau" NBER.org (April 2024).

Further, Lawrence Glickman wrote in "How White Backlash Controls American Progress: Backlash Dynamics Are One Of The Defining Patterns Of The Country's History" The Atlantic (21 May 2020), "The word, "backlash," gained popularity in the summer of 1963, when, after dallying on the issue for the first two years of his presidency, President John F. Kennedy proposed significant civil-rights legislation. In response, the word, which had primarily denoted the recoil of a fishing line, was repurposed, usually as "white backlash," to refer to opposition to the increased pace of African American civil-rights activism or the

Kennedy (and, after his assassination in November 1963, the Lyndon B. Johnson) administration's legislative proposals and executive actions, or both." Moreover, Catherine Comet and Mohamed Oubenal, "The Civil Rights Movement and Power Structure Research: An Interview with G. William Domhoff, "Who Rules America" UCSC.edu (24 May 2023)," G. William Domhoff remarked, "the Civil Rights Movement resonated for me because of my four years at Duke. Those years, 1954-1968, were years of total racial segregation of the oppressed and it came as a surprise and somewhat of a shock to live under those conditions, even though there was plenty of racial segregation of the oppressed in the North as well. The South felt very different to me, and I soon learned how brutal and callous most of my white Southern classmates were in their beliefs about oppressed Black lives. It was a situation of racial oppression that made me uncomfortable, but I did not fully come to grips with my thoughts about all this at the time. I was too focused on trying to achieve my own goals. Once the resistance to the Civil Rights Movement began, though, I knew that many white Southerners were fully capable of the violence they soon carried out against oppressed Black lives. I also believed there would have been even more bloodshed of oppressed Black lives if federal troops had not been sent into Southern cities at critical moments."

Again, there are those who argue that leaders as well as student-leaders and children in the Civil Rights Movement "failed." Yet, Leland Ware wrote in "Civil Rights and the 1960s: A Decade of Unparalleled Progress" Maryland Law Review (2013), "The legislation was a major accomplishment that met several of the goals of the Civil Rights Movement. The denial of access to places of public accommodation stigmatized and demeaned the oppressed. The threat of the loss of federal funding made racial discrimination in schools, colleges, and universities too costly to continue. The Civil Rights Act dramatically increased the educational opportunities available to Black lives. Racial discrimination in employment had relegated Black lives to the lowest paying, least desirable occupations. The Civil Rights federal law forbade employment racial discrimination. The 1964 Civil Rights Act did not address voting rights."

Brian Duignan wrote in "Voting Rights" The Encyclopedia Britannica (04 Jan 2025), "Voting rights, in U.S. history and politics, a set of legal and constitutional protections designed to ensure the opportunity to vote in local, state, and federal elections....This right to vote is an essential element of democracy in any country....and is one measure of how democratic a country is.....The Fifteenth Amendment of the Constitution guaranteed African Americans the right to vote. By the end of the nineteenth century, however, almost all the Southern states had enacted state laws which suppressed the Black vote."

Civil rights attorney, Yiyang Wu, remarked, "Of all the civil rights statutes that were passed in the '60s, the Fair Housing Act has some of the strongest language in terms of anti-discrimination." In "Why Fair Housing is Key to Systemic Equality" ACLU.org (05 May 2023), Sandra Park wrote, "Few fights are more pivotal to ending systemic inequality than the fight for fair and stable housing for the oppressed. When Martin Luther King, Jr. launched a campaign to end slums in 1966, he connected the struggle to obtain decent housing with the need to end what he called slum schools, work, health care, and all forms of racial segregation. Today, fair housing remains the key to addressing deepening income inequality and forced displacement from our communities, as the long-lasting reach of discriminatory housing practices constantly shape the lives of the oppressed who have access to quality education, health care, security, opportunity, and wealth." In "The Legacy of the 1968 Fair Housing Act" Social Forum (June 2015). Douglas S. Massey wrote, "The Fair Housing Act passed in the wake of Martin Luther King's assassination to address, at least symbolically, the anger of oppressed Black lives erupted in rebellions, revolts and uprisings in the nation's racially segregated and therefore poverty-stricken and resource-depleted ghettos. For the first time in American history federal legislation banned racial discrimination in the sale or rental of housing. At the time, levels of black residential segregation were extreme, higher than any group had ever experienced before or since." In addition, Douglas S. Massey wrote in "The Legacy of the 1968 Fair Housing Act" Social Forum (June 2015), Douglas S. Massey wrote. "Civil rights activists in 1968 hoped that the passage of the Fair Housing Act would lead to the residential desegregation of oppressed minority groups in American society."

CHAPTER 7

THE PROBLEM OF WHITE SUPREMACY, RACISM AND DEHUMANIZATION

It will be difficult, if not impossible to copy, to duplicate and/or repeat the Civil Rights Movement. This is because, leaders as well as student-leaders and children in the Civil Rights Movement came face-to-face with the contradiction and the problem of the myth of white superiority, the myth of Black inferiority, racism and dehumanization.

Arthur Schopenhauer wrote in "The Basis of Morality" (Hackett: 1840/1903), "The assumption that that the oppressed are animals are without rights and the illusion that our treatment of them has no moral significance is a positively outrageous example of Western crudity and barbarity. Universal care, compassion, concern, empathy, mercy and empathy towards the oppressed, is the only guarantee of morality." Thomas Merton remarked, "the Negro's plight is one calculated to antagonize him because it reflects such inability to see him, right before our nose, as a human being and not as a higher domestic animal...." Emile Cioran wrote in "Genealogy of Fanaticism' A Short History of Decay "(Arcade: 1949/2012), "Even when he turns for religion, man remains subject to it; depleting himself to create false gods, he then feverishly adopts them: his need for fiction, for mythology triumphs over evidence and absurdity alike ... We kill only in the name of a god or of his counterfeits: the excesses provoked by the gods. Reasons, by the concept of nation, class, or race, are akin to those of the Inquisition the Reformation." In "Mixing Christianity with Nationalism Is a Recipe for Fascism" New York Magazine (14 Sept 2022), Ed Gilgore wrote, "Conservative Christians....dehumanizing their many perceived enemies has become so common that cries of anguish from within the ranks of Evangelical Protestantism itself are become more pointed every day." It is reported that Captain Ibrahim Traore, President of Burkina Faso remarked, " "Don't talk about human rights. Because these people see us as subhumans. They see us as slaves. That's how it is in their minds. They have never changed their mindset..." The Freedom and Justice Institute wrote in "Why Is the White Church Questioning Black Humanity?" YouTube (07 May 2025), "James White is going to debate Corey Mahler as to whether or not black people can be sanctified to the same level as white people. Our question is, why are two white men debating black sanctification? However, the more alarming truth is that this debate is not over the sanctification of black people but our very humanity as white people." On the other hand, David M. Markowitz and Paul Slovic wrote in "Why We Dehumanize Illegal Immigrants" PLOS (07 Oct 2021), "Dehumanization is a pervasive social and psychological phenomenon that affects oppressed groups of persons in American society. Immigrants, for example, are viewed as less-than-human compared to the dominant group in the U.S. and therefore are treated inhumanely through cruel metaphors (e.g., immigrants are animals). Detainment policies also treat members of oppressed minority groups in dehumanizing ways by separating families at country borders and forcing people into poorly resourced detention sites...."

Leaders as well as student-leaders and children the Civil Rights Movement understood Howard Thuman who wrote in "Jesus and the Disinherited" (1949), "On the one hand, it is the sin of arrogance and pride that has tended to vitiate the missionary impulse and to make of it an instrument of self-righteousness a racial superiority in the other hand." Howard Thurman wrote in "The Fascist Masquerade" in "The Church and Organized Movements" (Harper: 1946), "To be American and Christian is to be but a little lower than the angels in heaven." Moreover, Howard Thurman wrote in "The Fascist Masquerade" in "The Church and Organized Movements" (Harper: 1946), "Hate groups have established "squatters rights" in the mind of believers because there has been no adequate teaching on the meaning of faith in terms of human dignity and human worth." In addition, in "The Search for Common Ground" (Friends United Press: 1971/1986), Howard Thurman wrote, "I do not mean to offend anyone's religion. Yet, according to the "Merriam-Webster Collegiate Dictionary," "A myth is narrative, a metanarrative, a story that is ostensibly historical but often forgotten." The task of myth is to explain the action, activity, behavior and conduct of institutions, organizations, structures and systems. And the task of myth is to explain the action, activity, behavior and conduct of natural phenomena."

Leaders as well as student-leaders and children the Civil Rights Movement understood Howard Thuman who wrote in "The Search for Common Ground" (Friends United Press: 1971/1986), "'Black is beautiful' was a phrase, a stance, a metaphysic and a total world view. In very exciting terms it undermined the myth that Black is demonic, dirty and ugly. Moreover, the phrase 'Black is beautiful' undermined the myth of white supremacy and whit superiority in American society." Howard Thuman wrote in "The Luminous Darkness: A Personal Interpretation of the Anatomy of Segregation" (Harper: 1965), "Racism is the actions, activities, behaviors, conduct and events discrimination and therefore injustice on the basis of race in American society." Leaders as well as student-leaders and children the Civil Rights Movement understood Howard Thuman who wrote in "With Head and Heart: The Autobiography of Howard Thurman" (Houghton Mifflin Harcourt: 1979), "As Morehouse College student-leaders, we were Black men in Atlanta when the State of Georgia was infamous for its racial brutality. Lynchings, burnings, and unspeakable cruelties were the fundamentals of existence for Black people. Our physical lives were of little value. Any encounter with a white person was inherently dangerous and frequently fatal. Those of us who managed to remain physically whole found our lives defined in less than human terms in American life."

Leaders as well as student-leaders and children the Civil Rights Movement understood Howard Thuman who wrote in "Deep River: The Negro Spirituals Speak of Life and Death" (Friends United Press: 1945/1978), "....the enslaved were made to become breeders for profits; children were separated from parents and from each other---in fact, from the beginning, the slave population was a company of displaced and dispossessed population. The possibility of ever seeing loved ones loved ones again was very remote." Howard Thurman wrote in "Deep River: The Negro Spiritual Speaks of Life and Death" (Friends United Press: 1945/1978), "Death was a fact, inescapable, persistent. For the slave, it was extremely compelling because of the cheapness with which his life was regarded. The slave was a tool, a thing, a utility, a commodity, but he was not a person. He was faced constantly with the imminent threat of death, of which the terrible overseer was the symbol' the awareness of the awareness that he (the slave), was only chattel property......It is difficult for us, so far removed in time and mood from those agony-ridden days to comprehend the subtle psychological factors that were at work in the relationship between the slave and the master. If a slave were killed it was merely a property loss, a matter of bookkeeping."

Similarly, Caitlin Rosenthal wrote in "Accounting for Slavery: Masters and Management" (Harvard Univ. Press: 2018), "....many planters in the American South and the West Indies shared our obsession with data. They sought to determine how much labor their slaves could perform in a given amount of time, and they pushed their slaves to achieve that maximum. Many kept extensive records---account books and reports that reflect their experimental and often brutal, cruel, terrifying, and violent slave-management actions, activities, behaviors, conduct and practices." Howard Thurman wrote in "Deep River: The Negro Spirituals Speak of Life and Death" (Friends United Press: 1945/1978), "It is difficult for us, so far removed in time and mood from those agony-ridden days, to comprehend the subtle psychological factors that were at work in the relationship between slave and master. If a slave were killed, it was merely a matter of bookkeeping. To live constantly in such a climate makes the struggle for human dignity unbearably desperate...."

In "Deep River: The Negro Spirituals Speak of Life and Death" (Friends United Press: 1945/1978), Howard Thurman wrote, "Death was a fact, inescapable, persistent. For the slave it was extremely compelling because of the cheapness with which his life was regarded." In "Deep River: The Negro Spirituals Speak of Life and Dea (Friends United Press: 1945/1978), Howard Thurman wrote, "The slave was a tool, a thing, a utility, a commodity, but he was not a person. He was faced constantly with the imminent threat of death, of which the terrible overseer was the symbol; and the awareness that he (the slave) was only chattel property, the dramatization."

In "Deep River: The Negro Spirituals Speak of Life and Death" (Friends United Press: 1945/1978), Howard Thurman wrote, "....the enslaved were made to become breeders for profits; children were separated from parents and from each other---in fact, from the beginning, the slave population was a company of displaced and dispossessed population. The possibility of ever seeing love ones loved ones again was very remote." Howard Thurman wrote in "Deep River: The Negro Spirituals Speak of Life and Death" (Friends United Press: 1945/1978), "There was nothing more heart-tearing in that far-off time of madness than the separation of families at the auction block. In instance after instance, wives were sold from their husbands to become breeders for profit, husbands were sold from wives; children were separated from their families; a complete and withering attack was made on the sanctity of the family. Added to all this, the slave woman was constantly at the mercy of the mercy and the lust and the rapacity of the master himself, while the slave husband was powerless to intervene. Conversely, the slave husband was constantly at the mercy and the lust and the capacity of the wife of the master while the slave wife was powerless to intervene. Indeed, the whole sorry picture is a revelation of the depth of moral degradation...."

Remy Debes wrote in "Dignity' in "The Stanford Encyclopedia of Philosophy" (Spring 2023)," For the oppressed, dignity is a complex concept. In academic and legal contexts, it is typically used in the couplet "human dignity" to denote a kind of basic worth or status that purportedly belongs to all persons equally, and which grounds fundamental moral or political duties or rights.... for the oppressed, the concept of dignity has long been associated with many more meanings, some of which cut in distinctly different directions: rank, station, honor, uniqueness, beauty, poise, gravitas, integrity, self-respect, self-esteem, a sacred place in the order of things, supreme worth, and even the apex of astrological significance. Some of these connotations have faded with time. But most have an enduring influence." Helen Watt, Ph.D., wrote in "The Dignity of Human Life" CBHD.org (2020), "The concept, "value and worth of life" can refer to lives of the oppressed possessing inherent and intrinsic dignity, value and worth.... Human beings are equal in their basic ethical and moral importance.... respect for the dignity of members of oppressed minority groups is significantly impacted by a failure to value the very consciousness and existence of the oppressed in American society."

The Universal Declaration of Human Rights (UDHR), Article 3 states, all human beings are born free and equal in dignity and rights. They are endowed with reason and conscience and should act towards one another in a spirit of brotherhood; Article 2 states, everyone is entitled to all the rights and freedoms set forth in this Declaration, without distinction of any kind, such as race, color, sex, language, religion, political or other opinion, national or social origin, property, birth or other status. Furthermore, no distinction shall be made on the basis of the political, jurisdictional or international status of the country or territory to which a person belongs, whether it be independent, trust, non-self-governing or under any other limitation of sovereignty; Article 3 states, Everyone has the right to life, liberty and security of person; Article 4 states, No one shall be held in slavery or servitude; slavery and the slave trade shall be prohibited in all their forms.; Article 5 states, No one shall be subjected to torture or to cruel, inhuman or degrading treatment or punishment; Article 6 states, Everyone has the right to recognition everywhere as a person before the law.; Article 7 states, All are equal before the law and are entitled without any discrimination to equal protection of the law. All are entitled to equal protection against any discrimination in violation of this Declaration and against any incitement to such discrimination......"

In addition, Anna-Teresa Tymieniecka wrote in "The Notion of the "Human Person"" In "Logos and Life" (Springer: 1988), edited by Anna-Teresa Tymieniecka, "In contemporary thought the notion of the oppressed as a "human person" plays the role of a point of reference for understanding the human being. Human beings are in our times viewed in concrete terms, that is, not as an abstract model of an entity, but as a living individual struggling for survival with organic life conditions on the one hand, and world-conditions on the other. Concreteness and flexibility in the notion of the "human person" appear to be most appropriate for the accounting of various features of the human individual, which are approached from different perspectives. Fundamentally, this means: first, to grasp and indicate the distinctiveness of the human being with respect to other living individuals and things, and the modalities of organic and social life; second, to appreciate man's conduct, aims, and rights with respect to the perspectives of his innermost nature." Elaine Webster wrote in "Degradation," in "Humiliation, Degradation, Dehumanization," edited by Paulus Kaufmann (Springer: 2011), "It is assumed that the degradation of the lives of the oppressed expresses a particular form of violation of human dignity."

Paul Tiedemann wrote in "Philosophical Foundations of Human Rights" (Springer: 2012), "For the oppressed, according to its literal meaning "degrading" means to remove human beings from a relatively high grade or rank to a lower grade or rank....If a human being is captured and made into slave he too has been made into slave he too has been degraded....The language of the notions of cruelty as "inhuman" and "degrading," shows that there is no difference between their respective meanings. The meaning of both is to deprive the oppressed as human beings of their personhood." It is remarked that "Degradation" is the actions, activities, behaviors, conduct and events of lowering of the lowering the condition and status of the oppressed something to a less respected condition or state." In "Philosophical Foundations of Human Rights" (Springer: 2012), Paul Tiedemann wrote "For the oppressed, the attributes "inhuman" and "degrading" are synonyms. Both refer to humiliation by deprivation of personhood." Therefore, in "Philosophical Foundations of Human Rights" (Springer: 2012), Paul Tiedemann wrote, "A cruel act is an intentional act by which severe "mental" or "physical" pain or suffering is inflicted.... A cruel, inhuman, or degrading treatment takes place for particular purposes, seems to be considered the "torture" of the oppressed in all, any, each and every circumstance and context in American society."

In "Philosophical Foundations of Human Rights" (Springer: 2012). Paul Tiedemann wrote, "The cruel and hence inhuman treatment of the oppressed transfers them as human beings into a status of non-human beings. How is it possible to transfer human beings into a status non-human being? The oppressed as human beings are, by definition, living entities. Transforming human beings into something else can therefore mean to kill those human beings when it comes to oppression and to the oppressed, a convincing interpretation seems to be that "human" and "inhuman" is meant in an emphatic sense. In this emphatic sense, "human," is not merely that the oppressed are human beings but are persons. Cruel treatment of the oppressed is thus "inhuman," if such cruelty leads to the result that the oppressed as human beings are deprived of their personhood in American society." Moreover, Alba Papa-Grimaldi who wrote in What A Human Being Is" Funct Neurol. (19 June 2011),

"In all honesty the only answer I can find to the question when it comes to the lives of members of oppressed minority groups: "What is a human being?" is the Terentian adage: "Homo sum, nihil humani a me alienum puto. I am a human being who is being a human being": I consider nothing that is human alien to me." Nothing that can happen to a human being is foreign to me and makes me less human. Thus, neither happiness nor dignity are the definition of what a human life should be, but human life itself, for as long as it is recognized as such and cared for as such. Every other definition is and expresses the superfluous."

Ran Hirschl wrote in "Constitutional Theocracy" (Harvard Univ. Press: 2010), "How can a polity reconcile the principles of accountability and separation of powers and the notion of "we-the- people" as the ultimate and holy texts constitute the supreme governing norm of the state? Who should be vested with ultimate authority to interpret the divine texts, and on what grounds?" Henrietta Toth wrote in "Theocracy" (Rosen: 2019/2020), "The political system or type of government called theocracy is based on a religious deity, whose worship holds the highest power in matters of the state and in life." Henrietta Toth wrote in "Theocracy" (2019), that "Civil rulers govern in the name of God or a supreme being. Some theocratic rulers claim to have divine right and receive divine guidance." In "Theocracy" (2019), Henrietta Toth wrote "In a theocracy, the legal system is based on religious law, meaning the country's laws are determined and dictated by religion." Aaron Griffith wrote in "God's Law and Order: The Politics of Punishment in Evangelical America" (Harvard Uni. Press: 2020), "From the nation's founding to the early twentieth century, religious conceptions of crime and punishment underwent shifts in aim and scope, each of which laid important groundwork for the anti-crime consensus. Religious influence in prison work, support for policing, and, most importantly, the racialization helped set the stage for the sacred war on crime."

For example, Howard Thurman wrote in "With Head and Heart: The Autobiography of Howard Thurman" (Friends United Press: 1979/1986), "After my father died suddenly when I was nine years of age, our next hurdle was to find someone to preach at the funeral. By chance—if there is such a thing—there was a traveling evangelist in town, a man named Sam Cromarte. I shall never forget him. He offered to preach at Papa's funeral. He did not need to be persuaded. We sat on the front pew, the "mourners' bench." I listened with wonderment, then anger, and finally mounting rage as Sam Cromarte preached my father into hell. This was a change to illustrate what would happen to "sinners" who died "out of Christ," as my father had done. And he did not waste it. Under my breath I kept whispering to Mamma, "He didn't know Papa, did he? Did he?" Out of her own pain, conflict, and compassionate love, she reached over and gripped my bare knees with her hand, giving a gentle but firm comforting squeeze. It was sufficient to restrain for the moment my bewildered and outraged spirit. In the buggy coming home from the cemetery, I sought some explanation. "Why would Reverend Sam Cromarte do this to my Papa? Why would he say such things?" I promised myself that when I became a man that I would never join a Christian church!"

George H. Taylor wrote in "Race, Religion, and Law" Maryland Law Journal (2006), "Black lives are vulnerable to being caught in the web of the criminal justice system for conduct that may not be similarly criminalized when committed by white Americans." Anthea Butler wrote in "White Evangelism Racism: The Politics of Morality in America" (Univ. of North Carolina Press: 2021), "In the nineteenth century, the term "evangelical" was about white Christian missionary work, spreading the gospel to the amoral, immoral, unethical, and virtue-less atheists, the agnostics, heathen, the heretics, the idolaters, the infidels, the nonbelievers, the pagans, and the unbelievers," typically accompanied by colonialism. Frantz Fanon wrote in "Wretched of the Earth" (Grove: 1961/2007), "…. The white Christian missionaries," who were arguably the first Christian nationalists, "as colonizers were never done talking about humanity as 'the image of God' and never stopped proclaiming the welfare of the whole of humanity as the 'image of God'. Yet, the white Christian missionaries as colonizers often inscribes the colonized subject with ideas and ideologies of backwardness for the white Christian missionaries as colonizers the colonial subject is therefore 'dehumanized'…and turned into an animal," absent, therefore, of any awareness, cognition, consciousness, feeling, and sentience whatsoever."

Miles T. Armany, et al, wrote in "Christian Nationalism and Political Violence" (Oxford: 2022), that "Christian Nationalism is the set of beliefs which blends a Christian religious understanding of America's Christian origins with nearly Christian "apocalyptic" views on future threats to that Christian American heritage." Matthew Willis wrote in "How Antebellum Christians Justified Slavery" Daily JSTOR.org (27 July 2018), "Baptist and Methodist churches "had" opposed slaveholding members in the early years of the Republic. These denominations' rapid expansion in the South, however, meant abandoning this position "in recognition that upwardly mobile members increasingly included slaveholders." Justification for slavery came with this growth and found its parallels in the biblical subordination of women. "Southern ministers had written the majority of all published defenses of slavery," Jemison reminds us. For these ministers, slavery not only had divine sanction, but it was also a "necessary: part of Christianity. This was because slavery was defined as akin to a marriage: the power of slave owners over slaves paralleled the power of husbands over wives and of parents over children." In "How Antebellum Christians Justified Slavery" Daily JSTOR.org (27 July 2018), Matthew Willis wrote, "........white Christian Southerners repositioned themselves from an acceptance of slavery as a necessary evil to defending it as a positive good."

For example, Nell Irvin Painter wrote in "Slavery: A Dehumanizing Institution"(Oxford: 2006), ""Slaves retained their humanity thanks to the support of families and religion, which helped them resist oppression. Nonetheless, slavery was a dehumanizing institution. Assaults on the bodies and minds of the enslaved exposed them to trauma that was both physical and psychological. By the end of the eighteenth century, branding, amputation, and other extremely brutal forms of punishment became rare as means of controlling slaves. But beatings continued, causing slaves' most catastrophic physical and psychological trauma. Every ex-slave narrative includes scenes of physical torture inflicted by owners (female as well as male), overseers, and fellow slaves forced to administer their masters' punishments. The narratives also comment on the emotional pain of parents, children, and spouses, forced to watch their kin being beaten. Artists have depicted the physical torture of slavery in countless images, such as "Slave Lynching" by Claude Clark (1915–2001). The enslaved woman's nakedness before a crowd of onlookers adds further humiliation to the physical pain of the beating."

In "Slavery: A Dehumanizing Institution" (Oxford: 2006), Nell Irvin Painter wrote, "In addition to physical injury caused by beating, slaves suffered from the chronic conditions caused by overwork, scanty rations, and insufficient clothing. Frederick Douglass recalled going barefoot and ill clothed all winter and suffering from frostbite as a child. Stealing food to stanch constant hunger earned many slaves a slave a whipping. Years of hard work, often in swampy conditions, left their signs within slaves' bodies. The skeletons of enslaved children and adults working in eighteenth-century New York City bore the traces of lesions denoting excessive, repetitive stress. The remains found in the African burial ground in lower Manhattan indicate that about 50 percent of New York's colonial Africans died before the age of twelve, and 30 to 40 percent of those children died in infancy. Many of the 40 percent of the skeletons in the burial ground belonged to preadolescent children and show the thickening of the skull associated with anemia and osteomalacia (weakening of the bones due to poor diet and nutrition). The skeletons' enlarged muscle attachments are attributable to the heavy loads children were forced to carry. The skeletons also show signs of arthritis in the neck bones and lesions on the thigh bones from muscle and ligament tears, caused by carrying heavy loads."

Moreover, in "Slavery: A Dehumanizing Institution" (Oxford: 2006), Nell Irvin Painter wrote, when it comes the centuries-long effort to dehumanize Black lives in America, "Some slaves suffered from what is now termed post-traumatic stress syndrome, and some inflicted their pain on their kin. But every slave was vulnerable psychologically, and every slave was at risk of falling victim to psychological trauma. The enslaved bore the brunt of emotional pain, but their owners did not escape unscathed." In "Conceptualizing the Biblical View of Curse (Gen. 9:25-27) as a Metaphor for Natural Resource Curse in Zimbabwe" (2018), Temba T. Rugwiji wrote, "The human race is cursed for the sin of disobedience on the part of Adam, from whom all humanity is believed to have derived (Gen. 3:15-19). Because of the sin of Adam, all human beings have inherited Adam's curses such as death and toiling in order to survive. Chase remarks that after Adam and Eve disobeyed God, their punishments brought disruption to manhood and womanhood. Curse is also portrayed as a consequence of murder."

In "Conceptualizing the Biblical View of Curse (Gen. 9:25-27) as a Metaphor for Natural Resource Curse in Zimbabwe" Old Testament Essays (2018), Temba T. Rugwiji wrote, "In the book of Genesis (9:18), we read that Noah had three sons: Shem, Japheth and Ham. Ham had four sons: Cush, Mizraim, Put and Canaan (Gen. 10:6). Canaan was cursed because his father had seen Noah's nakedness (Gen. 9:25). Noah said: "Cursed be Canaan! A slave of slaves, a slave to his brothers! Blessed be God, the God of Shem, but Canaan shall be his slave. God prosper Japheth. But Canaan shall be his slave" (Gen. 9:25-27)."Furthermore, in "Conceptualizing the Biblical View of Curse (Gen. 9:25-27) as a Metaphor for Natural Resource Curse in Zimbabwe" Old Testament Essays (2018), Temba T. Rugwiji wrote, "Some curses (or misfortunes) were pronounced on individuals or a nation. These include, for example, pestilence, consumption, fever, inflammation, extreme burning, the sword, blasting and mildew (Exod. 28:21-22). It appears that "cursing" was not exclusive in the Bible; that is, it did not only involve outsiders and or strangers as victims, but also one's own children. Hence, in Deuteronomy 21:23, we read that one who committed a crime worthy of death should be hanged on a tree, in which the "victim"/"criminal" is described as "cursed by God" (Deut. 21:24)."

Temba T. Rugwiji wrote in "Conceptualizing the Biblical View of Curse (Gen. 9:25-27) as a Metaphor for Natural Resource Curse in Zimbabwe" Old Testament Essays (2018), ?We also read in both Exodus (21:15) and Deuteronomy (21:16-21) that children would be cursed for striking their parents and for being contemptuous towards their fathers and their mothers."

Sergei Artemov et al wrote in "Justification Logic" in "The Stanford Encyclopedia of Philosophy" (Fall 2024), "One certifies knowledge by providing a reason, a justification. Hintikka semantics captures knowledge as true belief. Justification logics supply the missing third component of Plato's characterization of knowledge as "justified" true belief....Proofs are justifications in perhaps their purest form." For example, The Conversation wrote in "The 'Curse of Ham': How White People of the White Christian Faith Used the Biblical Story in Genesis to Justify American Slavery, 1619-1865." The Conversion (12 May 2024), "Of the many ways that white Christians have invoked the Bible to justify their actions, none has exceeded in cruelty in terms of the "Curse of Ham" to justify the Slave Trade, the Muddle Passages and Chattel slavery.... Here is the moment, as told in Genesis 9:24-25 (New King James Version): "So, Noah awoke from his wine and knew what his younger son [Ham] had done to him. Then he said: 'Cursed be Canaan. A servant of servants he shall be to his brethren'."

The Conversation wrote in "The 'Curse of Ham': how Whitte People of White Christian Faith Used the Biblical Story in Genesis to Justify American Slavery, 1619-1865" The Conversion (12 May 2024), "The statement, "Negroes will not rule over white people, typified by Charles Caroll's white Christian apologetic, "The Negro a Beast Or, In the Image of God?" (1849), was a Christian white supremacist racist phrase that perpetuated white racial stereotypes of Black lives based on white Christian racial hierarchy after Reconstruction in American society. George T. Winston (1901), another "Negrophobic" writer, claimed in "The relations of the whites to the Negroes" (1901): "When a knock ism heard at the door [a White woman] shudders with nameless horror. The black brute is lurking in the dark, a monstrous beast, crazed with lust. His ferocity is almost demoniacal. A mad bull or tiger could scarcely be more brutal. A whole community is frenzied with horror, with the blind and furious rage for vengeance."

In "The Black Man as Beast and Brute Caricature" (2024), the Jim Crow Museum Ferris.edu wrote in "The Black Man as Beast and Brute Caricature" (2024), "The brute caricature portrays black men as inherently, innately, and intrinsically dangerous, violent, savage, animalistic, destructive, and criminal -- deserving to be held accountable, disciplined and punished by death. This The Black Man as brute is a fiend, a psychopath, a sociopath, and an anti-social menace." In "The Black Man as Beast and Brute Caricature" (2024), the Jim Crow Museum Ferris. edu wrote, "Black brutes are depicted as hideous, terrifying predators who target helpless victims, especially white women." Charles H. Smith wrote in "Negroes Too Much Liberty?" (1893), "A bad negro is the most horrible creature upon the earth, the most brutal and merciless." Clifton R. Breckinridge, in "Speech of the Honorable Clifton R. Breckinridge: In Southern Society for the Promotion of the Study of Race Conditions and Problems in the South" (1900), a contemporary of Smith's, said of the black race, "when it produces a brute, he is the worst and most insatiate brute that exists in human form."

CHAPTER 8

THE PROBLEM OF LAW, VIOLENCE, SCAPEGOATS, TERRORISM AND IMPUNITY

I t will be difficult, if not impossible to copy, to duplicate and/or repeat the Civil Rights Movement. This is because leaders as well as student-leaders and children in the Civil Rights Movements came face-to-face with the contradiction and the problem of law, violence, scapegoats, terrorism and impunity.

Leaders as well as student-leaders and children in the Civil Rights Movements understood Howard Thurman who wrote in "Deep is the Hunger: Meditations for Apostles of Sensitiveness" (Harper & Brothers: 1956), "Violence at first is very efficient, very effective, when it comes to oppression. It stampedes, overruns, pushes aside and carries the day. It becomes a major vehicle of power, or of the radial threat of power. It inspires fear and resistance. The fact that it inspires fear in the lives of protestors is overestimated. This is the secret of its deception." In addition, Howard Thurman wrote in "Deep is the Hunger: Meditations for Apostles of Sensitiveness" (Harper & Brothers: 1956), "Violence is the ritual and the etiquette of oppressors and are those who stand in a position of control in the world of the oppressed.... violence drives the oppressed, it makes them seek for cover, if they cannot overcome it in other ways."

Leaders as well as student-leaders and children in the Civil Rights Movements understood Howard Thurman who wrote in "The Luminous Darkness: A Personal Interpretation of the Anatomy of Segregation" (Harper & Row: 1965), "Both the creators of law and the enforcers of the law are white.... Thus, my mind does a double-take before I ask a police officer for directions on any street in American society." Further, leaders as well as student-leaders and children in the Civil Rights Movements understood Howard Thurman who wrote in "The Luminous Darkness: A Personal Interpretation of the Anatomy of Segregation" (Harper & Row: 1965), "From the point of view of power, the stability of the social order rests on its total acceptance. To this end, the ancient role of the scapegoat is called into play concerning members of oppressed minority groups in American society." For example, in "The Search for Common Ground" (Friends United Press: 1971/1986), Howard Thurman wrote, "The heart-rending years when countless Negroes from being lynched, burned alive and butchered with impunity by white me whose women and children are often special spectators of the inhuman ceremonies, rites and rituals across the United States are conveniently forgotten."

For instance, Jorge E. Viñuales wrote in "Crimes against the Oppressed and the Problem of Impunity "Minnesota of Law & Inequality (June 2007). "For the oppressed everywhere, the most authoritative characterization of the term impunity so far is probably the one given by Louis Joinet, the U.N. Special Rapporteur on the question of the impunity of perpetrators of violations of human rights....In his 1996 Report to the Sub Commission on Prevention of Discrimination and Protection of Oppressed Minority Groups," Mr. Joinet introduced the following concept of impunity: "Impunity means the impossibility, de jure or de facto, of bringing the perpetrators of civil and human rights violations to account – whether in criminal, civil, administrative or disciplinary proceedings - since they are not subject to any inquiry that might lead to them being accused, arrested, tried and, if found guilty, convicted, in a society." In addition, Jan Willem Wieland and Jojanneke Vanderveen wrote in "Crimes Inflicted Upon the Oppressed and Indifference as Excuse," Interdisciplinary Journal of Philosophy (05 June 2023), "According to an influential view, 'the amount of blame the oppressors deserve for inflicting crimes upon the oppressed varies with the extent of their indifference'. That is, the more wrongdoers act from a lack of moral concern, the more they would be blameworthy, after inflicting crimes upon the oppressed, in American society."

Ralph Lemke wrote in "Genocide" American Scholar (April 1946), "For the oppressed, genocide has two phases: one, destruction of the national pattern of the oppressed group; the other, the imposition of the national pattern of the oppressor. This imposition, in turn, may be made upon the oppressed population which is allowed to remain or upon the territory alone, after removal of the population and the colonization by the oppressor's own nationals." For example, Wikipedia.org wrote in "W.E.B. Du Bois and the Civil Rights Congress (CRC): We Charge Genocide" (10 Feb 2025), "We Charge Genocide" is a paper accusing the United States government of genocide based on the United Nation Genocide Convention. This paper was written by the Civil Rights Congress (CRC) and presented to the United Nations at meetings in Paris in December 1951..."

Richard Hofstadter and Michael Wallace wrote in "American Violence: A Documentary History" (Knopf: 1970), "Today we are not only aware of our own violence; we are frightened by it. We are now quite ready to see that there is far more violence in our national heritage than our proud, sometimes smug, national self-image admits." Richard Hofstadter and Michael Wallace wrote in "American Violence: A Documentary History" (Knopf: 1970), "What is most exceptional about the Americans is not the voluminous record of their violence, but their extraordinary ability, in the face of that record, to persuade themselves that they are among the best-behaved and best regulated of peoples. Violence is endemic in our history." Further, in "American Violence: A Documentary History" (Knopf: 1970), Richard Hofstadter and Michael Wallace wrote, "Violence is committed by isolated individuals, by small groups, and by large mobs; it is directed against individuals and crowds alike; it is undertaken for a variety of purposes (and at times for no discernible rational purpose at all), and in a variety of ways ranging from assassinations and murders to lynchings, duels, brawls, feuds, and riots...."

In "American Violence: A Documentary History" (Knopf: 1970), Richard Hofstadter and Michael Wallace wrote, "Violence, in American society, is various, diffuse, and spontaneous, and is endemic in our history. Americans, apparently taking it as a part of the stream of life's events, do not as a rule very promptly rise up in large numbers and in lawful ways to protest, oppose, or control it. They are legendary for their refusal to accept the reality of death, but violence they endure as part of the nature of things, and as one of those evils to be expected from life. Yet, we have a remarkable lack of memory where violence is concerned and have left most of our excesses a part of our buried history." Further, Vittorio Bufacchi wrote in "Two Concepts of Violence" Political Studies Review (2005), "The twentieth century has appropriately been defined as the long century of the exercise of power and violence against oppressed members of oppressed minority groups .... For every member of oppressed minority groups person killed by an act of violence there are many more who have survived barbarism, torture, brutality, cruelty, persecution, the loss of loved ones, or (if they are lucky) the loss of all their belongings and livelihood."

In "Two Concepts of Violence" Political Studies Review (2005), Vittorio Bufacchi wrote, "The persistent proliferation of the exercise of political politic power and thus political violence upon the oppressed should not come as a surprise, given that the exercise of political politic power and thus political violence against the oppressed is, and has always been, the essence of politics in American society ....to paraphrase Max Weber's famous dictum on the State, claims a monopoly over the legitimate use of violence against the oppressed. The exercise of political politic power and thus political violence force used by state institutions may be legal, even legitimate, but it is still violence. And when the state is incapable of providing protection for members of oppressed minority groups, private agencies, as well as private actors, will take over the role of dispensing violence and security." Johan Galtung wrote in "Violence, Peace, and Peace Research" Journal of Peace Research (1969), "The oppressor may win the game of force over the oppressed. But not the moral issue - and when that dawns upon him and his allies, change of consciousness sets in, and demoralization starts thawing the frozen heart. The game is over." Johan Galtung wrote in "Violence, Peace, and Peace Research" Journal of Peace Research (1969), "When it comes to members of oppressed minority groups, the killed are dead, the bereaved are traumatized. The trauma may be converted to hatred that may be converted into revenge addiction."

In "Violence, Peace, and Peace Research" Journal of Peace Research (1969), Johan Galtung wrote, "Manifest violence," whether collective, personal or structural, is observable, although not directly since the theoretical entity of 'potential realization' also enters the picture. "Latent violence" is something which is not there yet might easily come about ... structural about, structural violence becomes apparent because it stands out like an enormous rock in a creek, impeding the free flow, creating all kinds of eddies and turbulences." Moreover, Johan Galtung wrote in "Violence, Peace, and Peace Research" Journal of Peace Research (1969), "In other words, we conceive of structural violence, which is inflicted upon members of oppressed minority groups, as something that shows a certain stability, whereas personal violence (e. g. as measured by the tolls caused by group conflict in general and war in particular) shows tremendous fluctuations over time."

Allison Rutherford et al wrote in "Violence: A Glossary" NIH.gov (Aug 2007), "Violence is defined by the World Health Organization in the WRVH as "the intentional use of physical force or power, threatened or actual, against oneself, another person, or against members of oppressed minority group or members of oppressed communities, that either results in or has a high likelihood of resulting in injury, death, psychological harm, maldevelopment or deprivation." See Krug E, Dahlberg L, Mercy J.et al "World Report on Violence and Health" (Geneva: World Health Organization: 2002). Further, in "Violence: A Glossary" NIH.gov (Aug 2007), Allison Rutherford et al wrote. "This definition emphasizes that oppressors who are in power must intend to use force or power against the oppressed in order for an act to be classified as violent. Violence is thus distinguished from injury or harm that results from unintended actions and incidents. This definition also draws attention not only to the use of physical force but also to the use of threatened or actual power. Such power or force may be used against oneself, against an individual or against a group or community, as in gang violence or repression of ethnic groups. When it comes to oppressors and the oppressed, violence is here defined not only as resulting in physical injury but as being present where psychological harm, maldevelopment or deprivation occurs; acts of omission or neglect, and not only of commission, can therefore be categorized as violent."

In "The Problem of State Violence" American Academy of Arts & Sciences (2022), Paul Butler wrote, "It is easy to see state violence in the U.S. Department of Defense "1033 Program," which provides "surplus" military equipment like armored tanks, grenade launchers, and bayonets for local police departments to use against members of oppressed minority groups. Likewise, many recognize state violence in the facts that police use of force is the sixth leading cause of death of men between the ages of twenty-five and twenty-nine, and that one in one thousand oppressed Black men are killed by the state sanctioned violence of police in American society." In "Police Violence Is Also Political Violence---and Deeply Normalized in the U.S." Truth Out.org (16 July 2024), Lewis Raven Wallace wrote, "the sun rises and sets over an America in which a different form of political violence – police violence – is normalized in every sense of the word. The grief and rage of countless families and communities sits in the darkness of that reality."

In "Police Brutality: From the Civil Rights Movement to Today, little has Changed" Union College.edu (n.d.), Trace Whalen wrote, "Black lives have always been oppressed by whites, and while that oppression may have transformed over time, it is still present today. Following the 1896 U.S. Supreme Court case "Plessy v Ferguson," which legalized the Jim Crow laws of racial segregation under the motto 'separate but equal,' almost everything, including school systems, was racially segregated. It was not until the U.S. Supreme Court case "Brown v Board of Education "in 1954 when racially segregated education was deemed unconstitutional. Still, racial segregation was incorporated in daily life until the Civil Rights Act was signed by President Lyndon B. Johnson in 1964. While segregation and race related laws have been abolished, police officers, as well as other branches of the law enforcement system, have been notorious for finding ways to continue to suppress African Americans. While the Civil Rights Movement and movements in more recent years have been effective in eradicating segregation and racist laws and practices, Jim Crow has continued in the mass incarceration, police brutality, and other forces of systematic violence against African Americans. Since 1964, police and legal systems across the country have remained systematically racist."

In "The Lawlessness of Law: Lynching and Anti-Lynching in the Contemporary USA" Settler Colonial Studies (2025), Jesse Carr wrote,

"In the aftermath of the Civil War, both frontier lynching and pro-slavery lynching re-emerged in new forms, and the institution of lynching began to regain the legitimacy that it lost during the strife of the prewar decades, reinvigorated by the closing of the frontier in the 1880s and 1890s. In the west, lynching was used as part of the domination of indigenous and migrant populations in order to claim meaningful sovereignty over newly acquired lands. In the south, along with disenfranchisement and economic exploitation, lynching reestablished pre-abolition racial hierarchies. This represented a key moment in the history of lynching, when the coexistence of frontier lynching in the west and racialized post-Reconstruction lynching in the south fueled. In both arenas, the violence involved with lynching escalated, while the reasons a person might be lynched were increasingly petty."

Moreover, leaders as well as student-leaders and children in the Civil Rights Movement understood Howard Thurman who wrote in "The Luminous Darkness: A Personal Interpretation of the Anatomy of Segregation" (Harper & Row: 1965), "The law tends to treat the Negro different from how it treats a white person. This is what makes the pattern of injustice towards the oppressed effective in American society." For example, Joshua C. Thurow wrote in "Atonement" in "The Stanford Encyclopedia of Philosophy" (Summer 2023), "Atonement is what oppressors do to fix relationships fractured by wrongdoing. To atone is, at first pass, to do something to repair this rupture by addressing the source of the rupture, namely the wrongdoing. The end goal is to become one, to be at one, or to reconcile. "Making amends" is often used to describe what is done to repair the rupture. Atonement is a particularly prominent concept within Judaism and Christianity, which hold that humans must atone for their sins against God. The Christian doctrine of the atonement states that Christ has atoned for the sins of the oppressors."

Michael Bauer et al wrote in "Shifting Punishment onto Minorities: Experimental Evidence of Scapegoating" Economic Journal (2023), "Scapegoating to a social phenomenon where members of aggrieved, angry, offended and resentment-filled dominant groups with power, take revenge upon members of oppressed minority groups. in the same society. Thus, we see those members of oppressed minority groups often suffer and atone for the wrongdoing members of aggrieved, angry, offended and resentment-filled dominant groups with power, and through this method of subjugation, and are presented as the group that is in the wrong and that must justify their existence through their atonement...." In "Making Amends: Atonement in Morality, Law, and Politics" (Oxford: 2009/2011), Linda Radzik wrote, "Our moral theories should tell us not just what is right and wrong, concerning oppressed minority groups, but also how to deal with wrongdoing once it occurs... a proper understanding of the correction of wrongdoing requires a proper understanding of wrongdoing, one that included a comprehensive view of the nature, consequences, and symbolic power of wrongdoing."

Moreover, in "Scapegoats" (Fortress Press: 2022), Jennifer Garcia Bashaw wrote,"....it was white Christian men, white Christian women, and white Christian children, pastors, deacons, and laypersons, who were behind the scapegoating, terrorism, torture, and violence that was....the spectacle lynching, burning alive, and butchering of unarmed and therefore defenseless Black men with legal impunity and with legal impunity, for 100 years in 48 out of 50 states in the union, after the end of the Civil War in 1865 and after the end of Reconstruction in 1877."

In "Terror in the Theory of Revolution" in "Terrorism, Ideology and Revolution" (Avalon: 1986/2019), Peter Calvert wrote, "Terror is the institutional, organizational, structural and systematic use of fear...." In "Terrorism, Political Extremism, and Crime and Criminal Justice" Annual Review of Criminology (2024), ""For the FBI's purposes, domestic terrorism is defined by 18 U.S.C. § 2331(5) as activities: 1) Involving acts dangerous to human life that are a violation of the criminal laws of the United States or of any state; 2) Appearing to be intended to: Intimidate or coerce a civilian population; Influence the policy of government by intimidation or coercion; or affect the conduct of a government by mass destruction, assassination or kidnapping; and 3) Occurring primarily within the territorial jurisdiction of the United States...."

In addition, Jeff Victoroff wrote in "The Mind of the Terrorist" Journal of Conflict Resolution (February 2005), "Most terrorists belong to groups exhibiting some or all of the hierarchical levels of authority.... most of the literature attributing clinical mental disorder to terrorists speaks of the remorseless personality type, psychopathy or sociopathy, for example, states that terrorists, like psychopaths, are ruthless.: In "The Causes of Terrorism" Comparative Politics (July 1981), Martha

Crenshaw wrote, "Terrorist violence communicates a political message; its ends go beyond damaging an enemy's material resources. The targets or objects of terrorist attacks have little intrinsic value to the terrorist group but represent a larger human audience whose reaction the terrorists seek." Martha Crenshaw wrote in "The Causes of Terrorism" Comparative Politics (July 1981), "We approach terrorism as a form of political behavior resulting from the deliberate choices of basically rational actors...." Amet Guler et al wrote in "Deconstructing Fears of Terrorism" Terrorism and Political Violence (2024), Terrorist attacks commonly create fear among individuals exposed to these acts due to their violent, brutal, and destructive strategies. Terrorist organizations aim to infuse fear and panic among the public.... "

Rachel Yehuda and Steven Hyman wrote in "The Impact of Terrorism on Brain, and Behavior: What We Know and What We Need to Know. Neuropsychopharmacology (2005), "Following the terrorist attacks, there are reported symptoms such as difficulties paying attention at work or school, depressed feelings, disrupted sleep, and anger.... the psychological impact of terrorist acts and threats can be widespread." In "Practicing What They Preach? Lynching and Religion in the American South" AJS (2013), Amy Kate Bailey and Karen A. Snedker wrote, "The link between lynching and race is unquestionable, particularly within the American South. At least 2,500 Blacks are known to have been so murdered in former Confederate States during the lynching era – a rate of roughly one mob killing every week for five decades. While lynchings occurred throughout the United States in the late 19th and early 20th centuries... The practice was substantially more frequent in the South and 90% of Southern victims were African American. Of the victims in lynching inventory, 94% died at the hands of white lynch mobs."

Moreover, in "Practicing What They Preach? Lynching and Religion in the American South" AJS (2013), Amy Kate Bailey and Karen A. Snedker wrote, "The link between lynching and race is unquestionable, particularly within the American South. At least 2,500 Blacks are known to have been so murdered in former Confederate States during the lynching era – a rate of roughly one mob killing every week for five decades. While lynchings occurred throughout the United States in the late 19th and early 20th centuries... The practice was substantially more frequent in the South and 90% of Southern victims were African

American. Of the victims in lynching inventory, 94% died at the hands of white lynch mobs."

In "At the Altar of Lynching: The Burning of Sam Hose in the American South" (Cambridge Univ. Press: 2018), Donald G. Mathews wrote, "On the third Sunday after Easter in 1899, about forty miles southwest of Atlanta near Newman, Georgia, a white crowd burned to death a Black laborer named Sam Hose. The atrocity blended anger, brutality, festivity, and satisfaction into a mood just beyond comprehension. "Glory!" shouted an excited man enraptured by the intensity of the moment, "Glory be to God!"" The signs that the scapegoating tactic that has been used by people in power is working are apparent and are signaled by multitudes of observations such as this. It displays to us that these people really and truly believe that they are working for the good of society and the people since this sort of thinking -Black people being evil, unclean, unruly, sinful- has been so deeply ingrained into their psyche."

Further, James W. Clarke wrote in "Without Fear or Shame: Lynching, Capital Punishment and the Subculture of Violence in the American South" (Cambridge University Press: 1998), "Recent studies of lynching have focused on structural theories that have been tested with demographic, economic and electoral data without much explanatory success. This article suggests that lynching was largely a reflection of a facilitating subculture of violence within which these atrocities were situationally determined by cultural factors not reported in census and economic tabulations, or election returns. Lynching declined in the twentieth century, in part, as a result of segregation and disfranchisement policies, but mainly because state executioners replaced lynch mobs in carrying out the will of the white majority." In "How White Americans Used Lynchings To Terrorize And Control Black People; The Legacy Of Such Brutal, Racist Murders Is Still Largely Ignored" (2018), James and Sam Morris wrote, "Historians broadly agree that lynchings were a method of social and racial control meant to terrorize black Americans into submission, and into an inferior racial caste position. They became widely practiced in the US east, north, south and west from roughly 1877, the end of post-civil war reconstruction, through 1950. A typical lynching would involve criminal accusations, often dubious, against a black American, an arrest, and the assembly of a "lynch mob" intent on subverting the normal constitutional judicial process. Victims would be seized and subjected to every imaginable manner of physical torment, with the torture usually ending with being hung from a tree and set on fire. More often than not, victims would be dismembered, and mob members would take pieces of their flesh and bone as souvenirs. In a great many cases, the mobs were aided and abetted by law enforcement (indeed, they often were the same people)."

In "How White Americans Used Lynchings To Terrorize And Control Black People; The Legacy Of Such Brutal, Racist Murders Is Still Largely Ignored" (2018), James and Sam Morris wrote, Police officers would routinely leave a black inmate's jail cell unguarded after rumors of a lynching began to circulate to allow for a mob to kill them before any trial or legal defense could take place." In "Documenting Reconstruction Violence: Known and Unknown Horrors" Equal Justice Initiative.org (2025), Equal Justice Initiative.org wrote, "For instance, between 1865 and 1877, countless oppressed Black men, Black women, and Black children were attacked, killed, massacred, murdered, terrorized and tortured by white mobs and persons who were shielded from arrest and prosecution. White supremacist domestic terrorists were never held accountable by the State. Instead, white supremacist domestic terrorists were celebrated in American life." In "The Southern Rite of Human Sacrifice Part III: Sacrificing Christ/Sacrificing Black Men" The Journal of Southern Religion (1990), Donald G. Mathews wrote, "Conceiving of God as Supreme Hangman and the Christ as Divine Substitute who paid the penalty for human sin in blood sacrifice did not make Christians lynch Black men. The formula did, however, reflect a state of mind; it reflected the ways in which moral accountability and penalty could allow ... violence against a Black man...."

Equal Justice Initiative.org wrote in "Documenting Reconstruction Violence: Known and Unknown Horrors" Equal Justice Initiative.org (2025), "Whether the State was dealing with slaves or freedmen, courts and jurists seldom wavered from the urgent need to solidify white supremacy, ensure the proper discipline and punishment of oppressed Blacks, and to severely discipline and punish severely the oppressed who violated the racial code . . . After their initial experiences with the judicial system of the State, many oppressed freedmen found little reason to place any confidence in it. As State laws discriminated against the oppressed, the courts upheld a double standard of justice, and the police acted as the enforcers." Moreover, Equal Justice Initiative.org wrote in "Documenting Reconstruction Violence: Known and Unknown Horrors" Equal Justice Initiative.org (2025), "The new era of Reconstruction offered great promise for oppressed Black lives. However, it quickly became clear that "emancipation" in the United States did not mean "equality" for oppressed Black lives without guaranteed and protected freedoms, liberties and rights for the oppressed. Therefore, the hope of Reconstruction (1865-1877) offered great hope for the oppressed but quickly became a nightmare if "unique," "unprecedented," and "unparalleled" State-allowed and/or State-sanctioned physical terrorism and physical violence and hence oppression across the entire landscape of American society."

Equal Justice Initiative.org wrote in "Documenting Reconstruction Violence: Known and Unknown Horrors" Equal Justice Initiative. org (2025), "Whether the State was dealing with slaves or freedmen, courts and jurists seldom wavered from the urgent need to solidify white supremacy, ensure the proper discipline and punishment of the oppressed, blacks, and to severely discipline and punish severely the oppressed who violated the racial code . . . After their initial experiences with the judicial system of the State, many oppressed freedmen found little reason to place any confidence in it. As State laws discriminated against the oppressed, the courts upheld a double standard of justice, and the police acted as "the enforcers.""

CHAPTER 9

THE PROBLEM OF POWER CAPITALISM, OLIGARCHS, DICTATORS AND CORRUPTION

It will be difficult, if not impossible to copy, to duplicate and/or repeat the Civil Rights Movement. This is because leaders as well as student-leaders and children in the Civil Rights Movement came face-to-face with the contradiction and the problem of the exercise of power.

For example, Martin Luther King wrote in "Where Do We Go From Here: Chaos or Community" (Harper & Row: 1967/2010), "....one of the problems the oppressed confront is their lack of power." Leaders as well as student-leaders and children in the Civil Rights Movement understood Howard Thurman who wrote in "Temptations of Jesus" (Lawton Kennedy: 1962), "A fundamental aspect of being a human being is the need for power in any society." Raymond Guess wrote in "Philosophy and Real Politics" Princeton Univ. Press: 2024), "In some central and important cases, ... the existence of specific power relations in society will produce an appearance of a particular kind. Certain features of society that are merely local and contingent, and maintained in existence only by the continual exercise of power, will come to seem as if they were universal, necessary, invariant, or natural features of all forms of human social life, or as if they arose spontaneously and non-coercion or by free human action of the oppressed in American life."

Leaders as well as student-leaders and children in the Civil Rights Movement understood Howard Thurman who wrote in "The "Will to Segregation" Journal of the Fellowship of Reconciliation (Oct 1943), "The "will to segregation "is defined as the exercise of power as authority, coercion, control and social control to restrict the movement in the Negro section of cities in American society." In "The Luminous Darkness: A Personal Interpretation of Segregation" (Harper: 1965), Howard Thuman wrote, "In American society generally formal power rests largely in the white community. In white society is the citadel of so-called power structure. The controls that determine the establishment and maintenance of law and order reside there. For this reason, prestigious members of the group can and often do function without social and moral responsibility..." For example, Daniel Costa wrote in "Citadel" The Encyclopedia Britannica (n.d.), "The concept, "citadel," is a fortified structure that is often located within a city or town. While designed to protect or subjugate social groups, citadels often played a significant role in shaping culture the word is from the Latin civitas ("citizenship," "the state," or "city") via the Italian cittadella ("small city")."

Peter Morriss wrote in "Power: A Philosophical Analysis" (St. Martin's Press: 1987/2002), "It is still deplorable when the oppressed are powerless but it also deplorable when the oppressed are dominated by their oppressors. To investigate how extensive is this domination---is to discover who is in the power of others." C. Wright Mills wrote in "The Power Elite" (Oxford: 1956), "In stark contrast with the oppressed, if we would understand the conservatism of very rich oligarchs, we must first understand the political economy of the power structure of the nation in which they become the very rich in American society." Further, Antonio L. Rappa wrote in "Power Structures" Government & Politics (2009), "All power is political. Power is the ability to convince, cajole, coerce, alter, influence, modify, or manipulate the actions, beliefs, or values of the oppressed. In other words, political power is about causing directional change or modification of the actions, activities, and behaviors of the oppressed.: Power structures are the vehicles with which such changes or modifications can be affected."

Moreover, Antonio L Rappa wrote in "Power Structures" Government & Politics (2009), "All power is political because it tends to be a spectrum of diversity, illusion, and abstraction whose effects can often be felt and seen but which itself cannot be touched because of its intangibility. As a result, there are competing definitions of power within a centuries old debate. There is a primary tenet in the study of political philosophy of power and power structures that is known as realism. Realist political philosophers define power in concrete and physical terms: Power is the ability of the oppressor to get the oppressed to do what the oppressed would otherwise not do. This realist view of political power...." In "Power Structures" Government & Politics (2009), Antonio L Rappa wrote in "Power Structure" Government & Politics (2009), "Power may also be perceived in terms of its symbols such as the head of state and head of government who thus govern the oppressed. These important political positions may at times be fused as in the U. S. president.... and in most Western liberal democracies...." In "Power Structures" Government & Politics (2009), Antonio L Rappa wrote, "Max Weber argued that the exercise of power is itself an action or activity on the part of one actor that was forced upon other actors within a system. We can therefore conclude that the success or failure of the strength of an actor's power is seen in the extent to which there is resistance to the force of power. If the resistance is strong, then it is said that the actors will prevail; if there is little resistance or the resistance is weak, then it may be said that the force of power in terms of the initiator's will does not prevail. Weber's primary contribution in terms of bureaucratic power was perhaps best captured in the image of the "iron cage," that arose out of his work on society and economics, which human beings cannot escape. For Weber the idea of bureaucracy was to control and extend the power of its occupants, and those who held office."

Moreover, Harold D. Laswell wrote in "Politics: Who Gets What, When, How" (Whittlesey House: 1936), "Politics is defined as the exercise of authority, coercion, control, deterrence, discipline, influence, power, punishment and social control with the conscious aim, foal and intent of to deciding and to determining who gets what when and how." Steven Lukes wrote in "Power: A Radical View" (Palgrave Macmillan: 1974), "Power is defined as exercise of power for, power over, and power to, always with the conscious and deliberate aim, goal, and intent of bringing about consequences." Further, Steven Lukes wrote in "Power and Authority" in "A History of Sociological Analysis" (Basic Books: 1978), edited by Tom Bottomore and Robert Nisbet, "Power involves the bringing about of consequences."

In "On Violence" (Harcourt Brace & Co: 1970), Hannah Arendt wrote, "Power is never the property of an individual; the political philosophy of power belongs to the oppressed and remains only so long as the oppressed remains together." Robert A. Dahl wrote in "The Concept of Power" Behavioral Science Journal (1971) "Some people have more power than others is one of the most palpable facts of human existence.... Because of this, the concept of power is as ancient and ubiquitous as any social theory can boast. If these assertions needed any documentation, one could set up an endless parade of great names from Plato and Aristotle through Machiavelli and Hobbes to Pareto and Weber to demonstrate that a large number of seminal social theorists have devoted a good deal of attention to power, and the phenomena associated with it. Doubtless it would be easy to show, too, how the word and its synonyms are everywhere embedded in the language of so-called civilized peoples over the so-called uncivilized oppressed, often in subtly different ways: power, influence, control, etc."

In addition, in "The Term Politics Reconsidered in the Light of Recent Theoretical Developments" IBSU Scientific Journal (2010), Valeri Modebadze wrote, "Power is the ability of different parties to achieve something together that/which they could not accomplish individually. This power governs politics according to David A. Buchanan, and Richard J. Badham. "Power, Politics and Organizational Change" (Sage: 1999)." Valeri Modebadze wrote in "The Term Politics Reconsidered in the Light of Recent Theoretical Developments" IBSU Scientific Journal (2010), "According to Jeffrey Pfeffer in "Power in Organizations" (Pitman, 1981), "power is a means of achieving desired goals and effects. Whereas politics is the practical domain of power in action and involves those actions, activities, behaviors, conduct and events through which power is developed and used in institutional, organizational, structural and systems social settings." Moreover, Valeri Modebadze wrote in "The Term Politics Reconsidered in the Light of Recent Theoretical Developments" IBSU Scientific Journal (2010), "There are numerous definitions in the academic literature of power and politics definitions highlight outcomes which, in the absence of power and politics, would probably not be achieved.""

In "Power: Critical Concepts" (Polity: 1994/2018), John Scott wrote that "In its most general sense, power is the production of causal conclusions, effects, and results for the oppressed." John Scote wrote in "Power: Critical Concepts" (Polity: 1994/2018), "...power, in its most general sense, is the production of causal effects." Dennis Wrong wrote in "Power: It Forms, Bases and Uses" (Univ. of Chicago Press: 1979/2017), "power is an actor's general ability to produce successful performances...."Moreover, Michel Foucault wrote in "Power and Knowledge" (Random House: 1980), "These can all be summed up in two words: power and knowledge the problem of power relations between oppressor and the oppressed with the political and economic power structures of society." Michel Foucault wrote "Power and Knowledge" (Random House: 1980), when it comes to the political philosophy of power, "These can all be summed up in two words: power and knowledge the problem of power relations between oppressor and the oppressed with the political and economic power structures of society."

For example, in "The Search for Common Ground" (Harper & Row: 1971), Howard Thuman wrote "......sovereignty does something more. It gives the citizen an integrated basis for his action, activity, behavior, conduct and events so that there is always at hand a socially accepted judgment that can determine for him when he is lost, when he has missed the way--that is, when he is out of community...." Daniel Philpott wrote in "Sovereignty" in "The Stanford Encyclopedia of Philosophy" (Fall 2024), "Sovereignty, though its meanings have varied across history, also has a core meaning, "supreme authority within a territory. It is a modern notion of political authority. Historical variants can be understood along three dimensions — the holder of sovereignty, the absoluteness of sovereignty, and the internal and external dimensions of sovereignty. The state is the political institution in which sovereignty is embodied. An assemblage of states forms a sovereign states system." In "State Sovereignty" (2024), J.E. Núñez wrote, "Whether the concept of "sovereignty" existed in the early years of civilization or not, the great thinkers in Ancient Western philosophy applied the notion to agents, bodies and institutions such as God, Emperors, Kings, nobles, people, law, and city-states.... clearly, regardless of the particular term used in a given historical period, the notion of "sovereignty" implies both power and authority. Depending on the degree of concentration or dispersion of power or authority, we may refer to the "state" or not."

Donald Black wrote in "Crime as Social Control" American Sociological Review (1983), "The sociological theory of social control predicts and explains how people define and respond to aberrant and deviant action, activity, behavior and conduct of the oppressed in fact, much of the conduct of the oppressed classified as crime in modern societies such as the United States is similar to these traditional modes of social control...." Megan C. Kurlychek wrote in "Social Control" Encyclopedia of Criminology and Criminal Justice (27 Nov. 2018), "Social control refers to the mechanisms through which a society is able to regulate and direct the actions, the behaviors and the conduct of the oppressed. These mechanisms take many shapes and sizes and are often classified by type and/or level. For example, social control is often divided into two types: informal and formal. Informal sanctions encompass such things as the oppressed not engaging in an action so as not to disappoint the dominant group in power. Formal social controls involve more direct action against the oppressed such as suspension from school or arrest and incarceration in the criminal justice system in American society."

The "Cambridge Dictionary" defines and describes the concept, "domination," as "the exercise of power or control over other persons, properties or things." Robert Litke wrote in "Domination and Other Kinds of Power" in "Philosophical Perspectives on Power and Domination" (Brill: 1997), edited by Laura Duhan Kaplan and Laurence F. Bove, "The specific kind of power that has received the most political and philosophical attention is "power over." Both the Random House Dictionary of the English Language"" and the "Oxford English Language" list it as a specific entry under "power." It is the ability to exercise governing, commanding, or controlling influence in a situation. I shall refer to it as domination or dominance." Further, Robert Litke wrote in "Domination and Other Kinds of Power" in "Philosophical Perspectives on Power and Domination" (Brill: 1997), "power is taken to be the central fact of political life in ant society....and when it comes to the political philosophy of domination and dominance "order" is the result of "submission to rules."" Nevertheless, the common cry of student leaders, as well as student-leaders and children in the civil rights movement was echoed in the words of Martin Luther King, who interpreted barbaric, brutal, cruel, dangerous and often deadly Jim Crow apartheid racial segregation laws, "An unjust law is no law at all. Therefore, we have a moral imperative to disobey unjust laws."

In "Domination" in "The Stanford Encyclopedia of Philosophy" (Summer 2018), Richard C. McCammon wrote, "Domination" is a kind of unconstrained, unjust imbalance of power that enables agents or systems to control other agents or the conditions of their actions. We can call this "the basic idea" of domination. The basic idea has the following components: 1) Domination is a kind of power, and usually "social" power—that is, power over other people. 2) Domination involves imbalances or asymmetries in power. The English "domination" comes from the Latin "dominus." A "dominus" is a master, and mastery represents an extreme of social power. Masters usually have all but complete control over how their slaves will act or over the conditions in which they act. As a result, the master/slave relation is often treated as the most obvious case of domination."

Leaders as well as student-leaders and children in the Civil Rights Movement understood Howard Thurman who wrote in "The Luminous Darkness: A Personal Interpretation of Segregation" (Harper: 1965), "Segregation gives rise to the amoral, immoral, and unethical use of power. Segregation is at once one of the most amoral, immoral, and unethical patterns of human action, activity and behavior. This is because the oppressed are outside of the magnetic field of ethical and moral concern. Therefore, it is always open season on the oppressed." In addition, Howard Thuman wrote in "The Luminous Darkness: A Personal Interpretation of Segregation" (1965), "Overt power is in the hands of white society. Well within its territory reside the controls. Therefore, it must always be remembered and never forgotten that the old saw that "power corrupts, and absolute power corrupts absolutely," remains true."

For example, Seumas Miller wrote in "Corruption," in "The Stanford Encyclopedia of Philosophy" (Winter 2023), "….one of the most popular of the standard longstanding definitions provided by Joseph S. Nye in "Corruption and Political Development American Political Science Review (1967), namely, "Corruption is the abuse of power by a public official for private gain."" Seumas Miller wrote in "Corruption," in "The Stanford Encyclopedia of Philosophy" (Winter 2023), "In fact, corruption is exemplified by a very wide and diverse array of phenomena of blackmail, bribery, extortion, lawlessness, money-laundering, nepotism, obstruction of justice, perjury, quid pro quo, real estate fraud, tax evasion, vigilantism, and witness intimidation among other actions, activities, behaviors, conduct and events as corrupt." In "Human Rights and Corruption" International Journal of Constitutional Law (22 Aug 2024), Julie Peters wrote, "Corruption, the misuse of entrusted power for an undue advantage, stands in complex relationships to human rights. Human rights primarily benefit the oppressed in "recognition of the inherent dignity" of each human being, to cite the Universal Declaration of Human Rights (UDHR)." In contrast, corruption is a systemic harm, posing threats "to the stability and security of societies, undermining the institutions and values of democracy, ethical values and justice and jeopardizing sustainable development and the rule of law," as the preamble of the United Nations Convention against Corruption (UNCAC) puts it."

In "The Rise of Lawless Power: A Book Proposal" The Yale Law Journal (16 March 2020), Charles Reich wrote, "Law is the preferred instrument for guiding and limiting the use of power. Law frequently attempts to regulate the use of power....Yet, all too often law becomes the captive of power, and in totalitarian countries law is frequently the preferred instrument of power. Law is based upon past practice whereas power is often the result of new creations."

Maurice Waite wrote in "Paperback Oxford Dictionary of English "(Oxford: 2012), The concept, "dictator" is defined as "the action, activity, behavior and conduct of an individual who rules over a nation with absolute power." For example, Howard Thurman remarked, "It is amazing to me that among the first community to be captured by the modern dictator is the intellectual community." Hannah Arendt wrote in "The Origins of Totalitarianism (Harcourt Brace Jovanovich: 1951), "Thinking itself is dangerous the ideal subject of totalitarian rule is not the convinced Nazi or the convinced communist, but the people for whom the distinction between fact and fiction no longer holds." Moreover, Noam Chomsky wrote in "The Responsibility of Intellectuals" (New Press: 1968), "If you are a ruthless dictator, then the intellectual is the most potent threat to your power, and you do everything in your power to silence him or her." Yet, Michael Rubin wrote in "Why Do Journalists and Intellectuals

Whitewash Dictators? "AEI.org (20 July 2021), "Josef Stalin. Mao Zedong. Fidel Castro. Ruhollah Khomeini. What do many of the most brutal dictators of the 20th century have in common? Adoration and obfuscation by the top intellectuals and by the top journalists of their time.... "

In "Paperback Oxford Dictionary of English "(Oxford: 2012), Julia Cresswell wrote in "Oxford Dictionary of Word Origins" (Oxford: 2021), "The concept, "havoc," refers to "A victorious army commander would once have given his soldiers a signal to start plundering: he would "cry havoc." The sense of plunder gradually passed into destructive devastation, and the army itself would "make havoc." Further, in "Oxford Dictionary of Word Origins" (Oxford: 2021), Julia Cresswell wrote, 'The concept, "misery," comes via French from Latin "miser" or "wretched" meaning to "fail to hit target." For instance, Howard Thurman wrote in

"Jesus and the Disinherited" (Beacon Press: 1949), "In the hands of a dictator, like Adolph Hitler, absolute power is exploited and consciously, deliberately, and intentionally turned to ends, goals, plans, and purposes that make for havoc and misery in any society."

James P. Kraft wrote in "Havoc and Reform" (Johns Hopkins Univ. Press: 2021), "In terms of havoc and misery, disasters are usually sudden and unexpected. They typically occur in the blink of an eye, a moment in concrete space and time. The disaster of havoc and misery are occasionally played out over a period of days, weeks, months and years." In "The Prince" (Univ. of Chicago Press: 1532/1988), Niccolo Machiavelli wrote, "For the dictator, it is better to be feared than loved, if you cannot be both. Therefore, for the dictator, any cruelty has to be executed at once, so that the less it is tasted, the less it offends." In "The Prince" (Univ of Chicago Press: 1532/1988), Niccolo Machiavelli wrote, "There is nothing more difficult to carry out, nor more dangerous to handle, than to initiate a new order of things. For the dictator, vengeance is necessary because he has enemies in all those who profit by the return of the old order..." In "Modern Dictators" (Plume: 1987), Barry Rubin wrote, "The American political tradition has a surprisingly contradictory attitude toward dictatorship. On the one hand, the framers of the U.S. Constitution assumed that governments were naturally prone to becoming dictatorships. Therefore, they divided power among institutions (executive, legislative, judicial) and jurisdictions (federal, state, and local) in a system of checks and balances to prevent an excessive concentration of power...."

In addition, Aristotle wrote in "The Politics, (Penguin: 1995), translated by Stephen Everson, "For the oppressed, the real difference between democracy and oligarchy is poverty and wealth. Wherever oppressors rule by reason of their wealth, whether they be few or many, that is an oligarchy, and where the poor rule, that is a democracy...... oligarchy has in view the interest of the wealthy in American society." The Editors of Encyclopedia Britannica wrote in "Oligarchy" (06 Feb 2025), "Oligarchy is the oppressive rule of both capitalism, government and religion by the few, especially despotic power exercised by a small yet rich and wealthy advantaged, prestigious, privileged group for corrupt or selfish purposes. Oligarchies in which members of the ruling group are wealthy or exercise their power through their wealth...." The Editors of Encyclopedia Britannica wrote in "Oligarchy" (06 Feb 2025), Aristotle used the term "oligarchia" to designate the rule of the rich and wealthy few unjustly over the oppressed which denotes government by the few in which power is vested in the best individuals.....a hereditary social grouping that is set apart from the rest of society by religion, kinship, economic status, prestige, or even language. Such elites tend to exercise power in the interests of their own class."

Again, in "With Head and Heart: The Autobiography of Howard Thurman" (Mariner: 1979/1981)," I majored in economics. But I could not consider myself educated until I was able to predict the effect of modes of production in "With Head and Heart: The Autobiography of Howard Thurman" (Mariner: 1979/1981), Howard Thurman wrote, "I majored in economics. But I could not consider myself educated until I was able to predict the effect of modes of production and consumption upon my life as a Black man in America." Again, Bob Jessup wrote in "Modes of Production" (Macmillan: 1990), edited by J. Entwell, et al, "Karl Marx used the concept of the ownership of the modes of production and consumption in two main ways; to analyze the economic base and to describe the overall structure of societies. Thus, he employed it to specify the particular combination of forces and relations of production which distinguished one form of labor process and its corresponding form of economic exploitation from another. He also employed it to characterize the overall pattern of social reproduction arising from the relations between the economic base (comprising production, exchange, distribution and consumption) and the legal, political, social and ideological institutions of the so-called superstructure." and consumption upon my life as a Black man in America."

For instance, as a economist, Howard Thurman wrote in "Good News for the Underprivileged" Religion and Life" (1935), "Greedy men who seek to possess more than their fair share of this world's goods, products and services." Malcolm X remarked, "We are living in an era of revolution, and the revolt of the American Negro is part of the rebellion against oppression and colonialism which has characterized this era. It is incorrect to classify the revolt of the Negro as simply a racial conflict of Black against white, or as a purely American problem. Rather, we are today seeing a global rebellion of the oppressed against the oppressor, the exploited against the exploiter. This is because you can't operate a capitalistic system unless you're vulturistic. You show me a capitalist, I'll show you a bloodsucker. And you can't have capitalism without racism."

Karl Marx who wrote in "The Capital: A Critique of Political Economy" (Penguin: 1867/1993), "Accumulate wealth! Accumulate wealth! This is Moses and the Prophets!"" In "The Communist Manifesto" (Communist Workers' Educational Association: 1828), Karl Marx wrote in "The Communist Manifesto" (Communist Workers' Educational Association: 1828), "In one word, for exploitation, veiled by religious and political illusions, it has substituted naked, shameless, direct, brutal exploitation." In "A Contribution to the Critique of Political Economy" (Charles Kerr: 1904/2018), Karl Marx wrote, "In stark contrast with the oppressed, the directing motive, the end and aim of capitalist production, is to extract the greatest possible amount of surplus-value, and consequently to exploit labor-power to the greatest possible extent, from the lives of the oppressed." Further, in "A Contribution to the Critique of Political Economy" (Charles Kerr: 1904/2018), Karl Marx wrote "For the capitalist oligarchy in American life the sermon always is accumulate, accumulate! That is Moses and the prophets!" Albert Einstein remarked "An oppressive oligarchy of private capital cannot be effectively checked even by a democratically organized political society because under existing conditions, private capitalists inevitably control, directly or indirectly, the main sources of information in American society."

Moreover, Karl Marx remarked in Ian Fraser, "Hegel and Marx: The Concept of Need" (Edinburg Univ. Press: 1998). "A house may be large or small as long as the surrounding houses are equally small it satisfies all social demands for a dwelling. But if a palace rises besides the little house, the little house shrinks into a hut...." Amartya Sen wrote in "On Economic Inequality" (Oxford: 1973/1997). "The relation between inequality and rebellion is indeed a close one...." Jean Jacques Rousseau wrote in "Discourse on Inequality" (Penguin: 1755/1985). "When the people have nothing more to eat, they will eat the rich."

Karlijn Hover et al wrote in "Greed" Pers Soc Psychol Bulletin (28 Dec 2022), "The recent increase in research led to consensus that the desire to acquire more is defining feature of greed, often referred to as an "excessive" desire or an "insatiable" desire... Greed is clearly related to materialism, maximization, envy, and self-interest as all reflect wanting more. Materialism entails a desire for material possessions to signal success in American life. Greed is not only felt for outcomes that signal success or status for oppressors but can also be experienced for nonmaterial outcomes such the power to further oppress the oppressed in American society."

Angus Stevenson wrote in "The Oxford Dictionary of English" (Oxford: 2010), "The concept, "inequality," is defined as "action, activity, behavior and events that lead to, produce and result in a difference in circumstances, conditions, degree, quality, quantity and size." John Scott wrote in "A Dictionary of Sociology" (Oxford: 2014), "At its core, the early formulation of the concept, "inequality," described the exclusion of Black lives lack of access to and participation in American society's economic, educational, financial, judicial, legal, legislative, political, religious and social institutions, organizations, structures and systems." United Nations.org wrote in "Concepts of Inequality" United Nations. org (October 2015), "Inequality—the state of not being equal, especially in status, rights, and opportunities1 —is a concept very much at the heart of social justice theories." United Nations.org wrote in "Concepts of Inequality" United Nations.org (October 2015), "Economic inequality refers to how economic variables are distributed—among individuals in a group, among groups in a population, or among countries."

Robert Saucy wrote in "Fascism" The Encyclopedia of Britannica" (19 Dec 2024), "According to Hitler, democracy undermined the natural selection of ruling elites and was "nothing other than the systematic cultivation of human failure." Joseph Goebbels, Hitler's minister of propaganda, maintained that the people never ruled themselves and claimed that every history-making epoch had been created by aristocrats. Primo de Rivera wrote that "our Spain will not emerge from elections" but would be saved by poets with "weapons in their hands." In Japan the Tojo dictatorship dissolved all political parties, even right-wing groups, and was reduced." In "Fascism" The Encyclopedia of Britannica" (19 Dec 2024), Robert Saucy wrote, "Before they came to power, Hitler and Mussolini, despite their dislike of democracy, were willing to engage in electoral politics and give the appearance of submitting to democratic procedures. When Hitler was appointed chancellor in 1933, he abandoned his military uniform for a civilian suit and bowed profusely to President Paul von Hindenburg in public ceremonies. In 1923 Mussolini proposed an electoral reform, known as the Acerbo Law, that gave two-thirds of the seats in Parliament to the party that received the largest number of votes. Although Mussolini insisted that he wanted to save Parliament rather than undermine it, the Acerbo Law enabled the Fascists to take control of Parliament the following year and impose a dictatorship...."

Howard Thurman wrote in "Jesus and the Disinherited" (Beacon Press: 1949), "The question of deception is not academic, but profoundly ethical and spiritual, going to the very heart of all human relations." Moreover, Howard Thurman wrote in "Jesus and the Disinherited" (Beacon Press: 1949). "The penalty of deception is to become a deception, with all sense of moral discrimination vitiated. A man who lies habitually becomes a liar, and it is increasingly impossible for him to know when he is lying and when he is not. In other words, the moral mercury of life is reduced to zero." In "Jesus and the Disinherited" (Beacon Press: 1949), Howard Thurman wrote, "Much of the constant agitation for guaranteed and protected freedoms, liberties and rights for the oppressed grows out of the morally degrading aspects of deception and dishonesty that enter into American society."

For example, Niccolo Machiavelli wrote in "The Prince" (Univ. of Chicago Press" 1532/2006), "Men are so simple and so much inclined to obey immediate needs that a deceiver will never lack victims for his deceptions.... A prince never lacks legitimate reasons to break his promise. The new ruler must determine all the injuries that he will need to inflict ruthlessly. He must inflict them once and for all." In "The Definition of Lying and Deception," in "The Stanford Encyclopedia of Philosophy" (Spring 2016), James Edwin Mahon wrote, "There is no universally accepted definition of lying to others. The dictionary definition of lying is "to make a false statement with the intention to deceive" (OED 1989)....The most widely accepted definition of lying is the following: "A lie is a statement concerning members of oppressed minority groups made by one who does not believe it with the intention that someone else s(hall be led to believe it," as Arnoald Isenberg wrote in "Deontology and the Ethics of Lying" Philosophy and Phenomenological Research (June 1964)."

Igor Primoratz wrote in "'Lying and the "Methods of Ethics" International Studies in Philosophy (1984), "lying is making a statement believed to be false, with the intention of getting another to accept it as true."" Further, Uri Gneezy wrote in Deception: The Role of Consequences" American Economic Review (March 2005), "the working definition of deception I use in this paper is: "A successful or unsuccessful deliberate attempt, without forewarning, to create in another a belief about members of oppressed minority groups that the communicator considers to be untrue in order to increase the payoff of the communicator\ at the expense of the other side."" Moreover, Alec Walen wrote in " Retaliation and Vengeance as Retributive Justice," in "The Stanford Encyclopedia of Philosophy" (Winter 2023), "Lex talionis" is Latin for the law of retaliation. It connects to the original retributive notion of paying back a debt, and it specifies that the debt is to be paid back in kind. It is reflected in the Biblical injunction.... to take "an eye for an eye, a tooth for a tooth" (Exodus 21: 23–25; Leviticus 24:17–20)." Similarly, Robert Nozick wrote in "Philosophical Explanations" (Harvard University Press: 1981). "Revenge involves a particular emotional tone, pleasure in the suffering of another, while retribution either need involve no emotional tone, or involves another one, namely, pleasure at justice being done."

Yet, there are limits to power. For example, Howard Thurman wrote in "Deep River: The Negro Spiritual Speaks of Life and Death" (Friends United Press: 1945/1978), ""Unless there is a great rebirth of high and holy moral courage, which will place at the center of the nation a vast power of an abiding sense of moral responsibility, both because of the nation's treatment of oppressed minority groups at home and our arrogance towards oppressed minority groups abroad, we may very easily become the most hated nation on earth. No amount of power, wealth or prestige can stay this judgment." Similarly, Marcus Aurelius wrote in "Meditations" (Oxford: 2020), "Looking back over the past, with it changing empires that rose and fell, you can foresee the future, too. Empires inevitably fall, and when they do, history judges them for the legacies they leave behind..." In "The Impending Collapse of the American Empire" Declassifieduk.org (18 June 2024), Chris Hedges wrote, "In the late stage of the American empire, the image sold to a gullible public begins to entertain the mandarins of the American empire. They make economic, educational judicial, legal, legislative, political, religious, social and theological decisions based not on reality, but based on their distorted, ideological, and mythological visions of reality, one colored by their own propaganda and character assassination of all, any, each and every oppressed dissent, doubt, agnosticism, cynicism and skepticism of American empire."

Moreover, Joseph Tainter wrote in "The Collapse of Complex Societies" (Cambridge Univ. Press: 1988), "Decline and disintegration of the social order of a society has been a recurrent concern in Western history... contemporary thinkers foresee the decline and the collapse of societies from such catastrophes as nuclear war, resource depletion, economic decline, ecological crises, or sociopolitical disintegration. Only recently have such fears become widespread. As Christopher Dawson has noted in "The Dynamics of World History" (Sheed & Ward: 1956), "Of all the changes that the twentieth century has brought, none goes deeper than the disappearance of that unquestioning faith in the future and the absolute value of our civilization which was the dominant note of the nineteenth century." In addition, in "The Collapse of Complex Societies" (Cambridge Univ. Press: 1988). Joseph Tainter wrote, "There is no point where a society can rest and say "Aha! We are sustainable!" It is something that always requires adjustment. Personally, I feel that when a society's narrative about the future includes the phrase "and then a miracle happens," that society is in trouble."

CHAPTER 10

THE PROBLEM OF PROPAGANDA AND CHARACTER ASSASSINATION

It will be difficult, if not impossible to copy, to duplicate and/or repeat the Civil Rights Movement. This is because leaders as well as student-leaders and children in the Civil Rights Movement came face-to-face with the contradiction and the problem of propaganda, character assassination both before and after death and was used to justify assassinations in American society.

Maurice Waite wrote in his "Paperback Oxford English Dictionary" (Oxford: 2012), "The concept, "propaganda," is defined as "the action, activity, and behavior of using biased, deceptive, false and misleading private and private and public discourses. Propaganda may be used to inspire violence against the oppressed; "violence" is derived from the Latin "ferox" which means "to be fierce, to be ferocious, and the condition and state of being barbaric, brutal, cruel, sadistic, and vicious."

It is reported, "After Burkina Faso took back control of its gold sector, a U.S. general used propaganda to assassinate the character of Captain Ibrahim Traoré by accusing Captain Ibrahim Traoré of misusing the profits. But many see it as a long-overdue move to reclaim sovereignty." It is reported, "In today's world, a bullet doesn't have to be fired to wound an African nation. All it takes is a clean, clever, and cruel headline as propaganda— to frame Captain Ibrahim Traoré as a radicalized communist, an extremist, a Marxist and a socialist."

Leaders, as well as student-leaders and children in the Civil Rights Movement understood Howard Thurman who wrote in "The Search for Common Ground" (Harper & Row: 1971), "Every doctrine of salvation involves propaganda and character assassination. This is because we do not know what to do with the unbelievers." Harold D. Lasswell wrote in "The Theory of Political Propaganda" (Cambridge Univ. Press:1927), "Propaganda is the management of collective attitudes by the manipulation of significant symbols. The word attitude is taken to mean a tendency to act according to certain patterns of valuation." Further, Harold D. Lasswell who wrote in "The Theory of Political Propaganda" (Cambridge Univ. Press: 1927), "The word attitude is taken to mean a tendency to act according to certain patterns of valuation. The existence of an attitude is not a direct datum of experience, but an inference from signs which have a conventionalized significance. We say that the voters of a certain ward resent a negro candidate, and in so doing we have compactly summarized the tendency of a particular group to act toward a particular object in a specific context. The valuational patterns upon which this inference is found may be primitive gestures of the face and body, or more sophisticated gestures of the pen and voice."

In addition, Harold D. Lasswell wrote in "The Theory of Political Propaganda" (Cambridge Univ. Press: 1927), "Taken together, these objects which have a standard meaning in a group are called significant symbols. The elevated eyebrow, the clenched fist, the sharp voice, the pungent phrase, have their references established within the web of a particular culture. Such significant symbols are paraphernalia employed in expressing attitudes, and they are also capable of being employed to reaffirm or redefine attitudes. Thus, significant symbols have both an expressive and a propagandist function in public life." Further, in "Propaganda" (Horace Liveright: 1928), Edward Bernays wrote. "Propaganda is a consistent, enduring effort to create or shape actions, activities, behaviors, and events with the conscious aim, goal, and intent to influence the relations of the public to an enterprise, idea, or group." In "How To Detect and Analyze Propaganda" (Townhall: 1939), C.FR. Miller wrote, "Propaganda is an expression of opinion or an expression of action, activity, and behavior by individuals and/or groups of individuals deliberately, intentionally, and purposely designed to influence opinions and/or actions, activities, behaviors, or events of individuals and/or groups of individuals with reference to predetermined ends."

Moreover, "Propaganda," wrote T.J. Smith, III in "Propaganda" (Bloomsbury: 1989), "Is any conscious and open attempt to influence the beliefs of an individual and/or a group of individuals, guided by a premeditated, predetermined, and preplanned end and characterized by the institutional, organizational, structural, and systematic use of irrational and often amoral, immoral, and unethical techniques of persuasion." In addition, T.H. Qualter wrote in "Propaganda and Psychological Warfare" (Random House: 1962), "Propaganda is the deliberate, intentional, premeditated, and preplanned attempt by some individual and/or group of individuals to form, control, or alter the assumptions, attitudes, beliefs, and convictions of other groups of individuals by the use of instruments of communication...." In "Propaganda: The Formation of Men's Attitudes' (Vintage: 1950), Jacques Ellul wrote, "Propaganda is a set of methods employed by an organized group that wants to bring about active or passive in the actions, activities, and behaviors of a mass of individuals, psychologically unified through psychological manipulation and incorporated in an organization."

Lastly, in "Propaganda and Persuasion" (Sage: 1986), Garth S. Jowett and Victoria O'Donnell wrote, "Propaganda is the deliberate, systematic attempt to shape perceptions, manipulate cognitions, and direct actions, activities, behaviors, and events to achieve a response that further the desired aim, goal, and intent of the propaganda." Virgie Hoban wrote in "Discredit, Disrupt, and Destroy': FBI Records Acquired by the Library Reveal Violent Surveillance of Black Leaders, Civil Rights Organizations" Berkeley Library.edu (18 Jan 2021), "It was the late 1960s, and J. Edgar Hoover smelled trouble. The status quo — hallowed by hate, sanctioned by Jim Crow — was beginning to crack. Behind the scenes, J. Edgar Hoover's Federal Bureau of Investigation was keeping watch. In 1967, the FBI quietly unleashed a covert surveillance operation targeting "subversive" leaders and student-leaders of the Civil Rights Movement, the Self-Defense Movement, and the Black Power Human Rights Movement, including the Black Panther Party, Martin Luther King Jr., Elijah Muhammad, Malcolm X, and many others. The objective, according to an FBI memo: to "expose, disrupt, misdirect, discredit, or otherwise neutralize" the radical fight for Black rights — and Black power."

In "The Most Dangerous Negro: Martin Luther King and the Federal Bureau of Investigation (FBI)," Brandeis University.edu (Fall 2018), Jacob Silverman wrote, "Today the FBI honors the Rev. Martin L. King Jr. and his incredible career fighting for civil rights #MLKDAY" (FBI Twitter). While made with good intentions, this January 16, 2017, tweet from the Twitter account of the FBI is nothing but ironic. During the 1950s and 1960s, along with leaders and student-leaders of the Courts Litigation Movement, the Civil Rights Movement, the Self-Defense Movement, and the Black Power Human Rights Movement, Martin Luther King Jr. rose to prominence, At the same time, he became the subject of a mass surveillance operation by the Federal Bureau of Investigation. These projects became collectively known as COINTELPRO, derived from Counterintelligence Programs." In "The Most Dangerous Negro: Martin Luther King and the Federal Bureau of Investigation (FBI)," Brandeis University.edu (Fall 2018), Jacob Silverman wrote, "The FBI employed various resources against King including, but not limited to the use of undercover operatives, wiretapping, covert listening devices or "bugs," forgery, and blackmail. COINTELPRO was a systematic effort to infiltrate and sabotage the endeavors of political organizations deemed threatening to national security…"

In "The Most Dangerous Negro: Martin Luther King and the Federal Bureau of Investigation (FBI)," Brandeis University.edu (Fall 2018), Jacob Silverman wrote, "Today, COINTELPRO is a cautionary tale of the abuses of government surveillance powers inflicted upon leaders and student-leaders of the Civil Rights Movement, the Self-Defense Movement, and the Black Power Human Rights Movement." Jacob Silverman wrote in "The Most Dangerous Negro: Martin Luther King and the Federal Bureau of Investigation (FBI)," Brandeis University. edu (Fall 2018), "Nevertheless, there is another story to be told regarding the FBI's conduct towards leaders and student-leaders of the Civil Rights Movement, the Self-Defense Movement, and the Black Power Human Rights Movement with a specific focus on King Under the leadership of Director J. Edgar Hoover." In "The Most Dangerous Negro: Martin Luther King and the Federal Bureau of Investigation (FBI), Jacob

Silverman wrote, "The FBI sought to fabricate a negative public image of leaders and student-leaders of the Civil Rights Movement, the Self-Defense Movement, and the Black Power Human Rights Movement such as King. Throughout the 1960s, the investigative strategies of the FBI became more radicalized as it utilized and perpetuated false stereotypes of leaders and student-leaders of the Civil Rights Movement, the Self-Defense Movement, and the Black Power Human Rights Movement in order to spy on and vilify leaders as well as student-leaders and children in the struggle for social justice for the oppressed.

In "The Most Dangerous Negro: Martin Luther King and the Federal Bureau of Investigation (FBI)," Brandeis University.edu (Fall 2018), Jacob Silverman wrote, "COINTELPRO was not just an attempt to destabilize the Civil Rights Movement, the Self-Defense Movement, and the Black Power Human Rights Movement. It was also a larger effort to criminalize leaders and student-leaders, such as Martin Luther King. by portraying them as the oppressive racial stereotypes they fought to disprove in American society." Moreover, Harry Enten wrote in "Americans See the Civil Rights Movement Icon Martin Luther King Jr. as a Hero Now, but that Wasn't the Case during His Lifetime" CNN (16 June 2023), "Martin Luther King, Jr., was a civil rights leader and an American hero. Almost every American adult (95% in CBS polling) believes he was an important figure in U.S. history. But it wasn't always that way. The fact that King is now beloved and has a national holiday commemorating his birthday wasn't something that obviously was going to happen during his lifetime. This shows us that often the fight for civil rights was unpopular at the time, and it only becomes popular retrospectively...."

On the other hand, in "If We Must Die: Armed Self-Defense during the Civil Rights Movement, 1954-1967" Swarthmore College.edu (Fall 2018), Martin Palomo wrote, "The characterization of the Civil Rights movement as a movement of pacifists is inaccurate. Many organizations and activists who practiced non-violence acknowledged the right to self-defense and many Black lives did actively defend themselves and non-violent activists. The Civil Rights movement was largely a success in part due to the incorporation of armed self-defense in nonviolent activism that deterred white racists from attacking black communities. In many instances, armed self-defense was informal and typically involved one person or a small group. As the movement progressed, black southerners began to evolve their armed defense efforts into more coordinated organizations that challenged white violence and pressured the federal government to enforce civil rights legislation in local and state communities. Black women throughout the Civil Rights movement also openly challenged nonviolent civil rights organizations to adopt armed self-defense, advocated on behalf of activists who adopted armed self-defense, and on many occasions practiced self-defense themselves."

Kevin Cokely wrote in "How MLK's Death by Assassination Changed Black People and Challenged America's Ideals" University of Texas.edu (28 March 2018), "What kind of country was America that it could produce the type of hatred that would kill a messenger of love and peace? If Rosa Parks' refusal to give up her seat was the spark that invigorated the civil rights movement, King's assassination was the psychological accelerant that threatened to permanently derail it." Kevin Cokely wrote in "How MLK's Death by Assassination Changed Black People and Challenged America's Ideals" University of Texas.edu (28 March 2018), "April 4 marks the 50th anniversary of the assassination of Martin Luther King Jr. From Lincoln to King, assassinations of political figures have been part of our country's history. The assassinations of civil rights activists Medgar Evers (1963), Malcolm X (1965) and Martin Luther King Jr. (1968) were a stark reminder to black people that the of freedom and liberation often came at the ultimate cost."

George Washington University.edu wrote in "A Study of Assassination" George Washington University.edu (n.d.), "Assassination is a term thought to be derived from "Hashish", a drug similar to marijuana, said to have been used by Hasan-Dan-Sabah to induce motivation in his followers, who were assigned to carry out political and other murders, usually at the cost of their lives. It is here used to describe the planned killing of a person who is not under the legal jurisdiction of the killer, who is not physically in the hands of the killer, who has been selected by a resistance organization for death, and who has been selected by a resistance organization for death, and whose death provides positive advantages to that organization." George Washington University.edu wrote in "A Study of Assassination" George Washington University. edu (n.d.), "Assassination is an extreme measure not normally used in clandestine operations. It should be assumed that it will never be ordered or authorized by any U.S. Headquarters, though the latter may in rare instances agree to its execution by a member of an associated foreign service. This reticence is partly due to the necessity for committing communications to paper. No assassination instructions should ever be written or recorded. Consequently, the decision to employ this technique must nearly always be reached in the field, at the area where the act will take place. Decisions and instructions should be confined to an absolute minimum of people. Ideally, only one person will be involved. No report may be made, but usually the act will be properly covered by normal news services, whose output is available to all concerned..."

In "A Study of Assassination" George Washington University.edu (n.d.), George Washington University.edu wrote, "Murder is not morally justifiable. Self-defense may be argued if the victim has knowledge which may destroy the resistance organization if divulged. Assassination of people responsible for atrocities or reprisals may be regarded as just punishment. Killing a political leader whose burgeoning career is a clear and present danger to the cause of freedom may be held necessary. But assassination can seldom be employed with a clear conscience. Persons who are morally squeamish should not attempt it..." For example, in "Minnesota House Democratic Leader Dead after 'Politically Motivated Assassination'" Minnesota Reformer (13 June 2025), Michelle Griffin wrote, "House Democratic-Farmer-Labor caucus leader Melissa Hortman, who was among the most influential Minnesota elected officials of the past decade, died on Saturday morning after a man impersonating a police officer shot her in her Brooklyn Park home.... Hortman's husband was also shot and killed......Hortman, who has two adult children, was first elected to the Legislature 2004 and served as House Speaker from 2019-2024. She lost two elections before winning, which she said gave her an understanding of what it takes to win swing seats and hold them." Michelle Griffin wrote in "Minnesota House Democratic Leader Dead after 'Politically Motivated Assassination'" Minnesota Reformer (13 June 2025), "Her speakership will be remembered as among the most consequential in recent Minnesota political history she guided the state through the pandemic before helping Democrats achieve a trifecta in the 2022 election. During the 2023 legislative session, she helped bridge the wide gulf between moderates and progressives in her caucus to achieve a historic legislative agenda...."

Again, it is now well known that many of the leaders and student-leaders in the Civil Rights Movement either attended and/or graduated from institutions, commonly referred to as Historically Black College and University's (HBCUs). It is also now well known that Howard Thurman also attended and graduated at the top of his class from Morehouse College, which is also an institution commonly referred to as Historically Black College or University (HBCU), which had a profound direct and indirect influence upon leaders. as well as student leaders and children in the Civil Rights Movement. Why and how did Howard Thurman provide a profound direct and indirect influence upon leaders as well as student-leaders and children in the Civil Rights Movement? The theory here is that Howard Thurman had a profound direct and indirect influence upon leaders, as well as student-leaders and children in the Civil Rights Movement.

Again, Juan Williams wrote in "New Prize For These Eyes: The Rise of America's Second Civil Rights Movement" (Simon & Schuster: 2025), "Today's social movements are dealing with new realities, yet the truth is that civil rights activism is never quite finished." Further, it is reported "Around 2,000 communities nationwide plan to protest....Data suggests protests in 2025 have increased compared to previous presidencies...." Yet, this work has clearly shown that it will be difficult if not impossible to copy, to duplicate and/or to repeat the Civil Rights Movement. This is because the Cicil Rights Movement was unique, unparalleled, and without precedent.

www.ingramcontent.com/pod-product-compliance
Lightning Source LLC
Chambersburg PA
CBHW051320120626
46547CB00015B/2318